Cover
Rainforest on the Gordon River
Photo Peter Walton

Insert
Tasmanian Tree Frog
Photo Dave Watts

THE·RAINFOREST·OF·TASMANIA

The Rainforest of Tasmania was produced by an editorial team representing the Working Group for Rainforest Conservation, which was established by the Tasmanian Government. The team comprised Jamie Bayly-Stark, Peter Boyer, Mick Brown, Ken Felton, John Hickey, Robert Shepherd, Paul Smith and Mark Stranger. The text was written by Peter Boyer and John Hickey, and design was co-ordinated by Mark Stranger. The Working Group wishes to thank Jean Jarman, Robert Hill, Fred Duncan and Tim Wardlaw for their expert technical advice, and the photographers whose names are listed with their work. Responsibility for the content of the book, however, rests with the Working Group.

The editorial team consisted of officers from the Forestry Commission and the Department of Lands, Parks and Wildlife.

FORESTRY
COMMISSION
TASMANIA

Production of *The Rainforest of Tasmania* was funded by the Forestry Commission.

Copyright© Government of Tasmania,
1987 All rights reserved
Design by Vision Design
Typeset by Creative Typographics
Colour separation by Photo-lith

Printing: Tasmanian Government Printer
National Library of Australia
Cataloguing-in-Publication Data
The Rainforest of Tasmania
Bibliography.
ISBN 0 7246 1520 2.
1. Rainforests – Tasmania. I. Tasmania.
Working Group for Rainforest Conservation.
333.75′09946

THE · RAINFOREST · OF · TASMANIA

Foreword		9
1	Introduction	11
2	What is Tasmanian rainforest?	13
3	Evolution of the rainforest	19
4	Where is Tasmania's rainforest? Who controls it?	25
5	Rainforest types	31
6	Animals of the rainforest	55
7	The ecology of the rainforest	69
8	Commercial uses	89

9	Rainforest management	105
Further reading		111

Appendices:

Appendix 1: Glossary of common names	114
Appendix 2: Checklist of the higher plants in Tasmanian rainforest	117
Appendix 3: Rainforest communities in Tasmania	124
Appendix 4: Where to see rainforest	126

▲
A rainforested gorge in the Great Western Tiers. *Photo Rob Blakers*

FOREWORD

The rainforest of Tasmania occupies an important place in the spectrum of features which give this State its unique and special character and this informative and beautifully illustrated book will be of great value to the general reader who wishes to increase his knowledge of its value, characteristics and scientific significance.

The book is a remarkably comprehensive source of information about virtually every important aspect of Tasmania's cool, temperate rainforest, including the various forms it can take, its ecology, its evolution from its beginnings in Gondwanaland to the present day, the animal species which are found within it and the plant species of which it is comprised.

The treatment of the sensitive issues which need to be considered when developing a rainforest management policy is well informed, refreshingly balanced and a good antidote to tunnel vision.

Recognising the special values of Tasmanian rainforest the State Government established the Working Group for Rainforest Conservation in 1984. This group was charged with identifying rainforest conservation needs and recommending appropriate measures. This publication is based on the collective expertise of the group and the information which it has gathered.

The authors have been most successful in keeping the book comprehensible and within the reach of the layman without lapsing into superficiality or reducing its authority. It will help to enlarge the community's understanding of the rainforest and stimulate in the reader a desire to learn more about this very special Tasmanian asset.

The editorial team, the Forestry Commission and the Department of Lands, Parks and Wildlife have produced a most attractive and valuable book of which they and all Tasmanians can be proud.

His Excellency the Lieutenant-Governor
Sir Guy Green

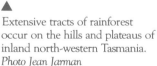

▲
Extensive tracts of rainforest occur on the hills and plateaus of inland north-western Tasmania. *Photo Jean Jarman*

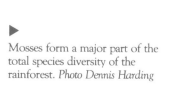

▶
Mosses form a major part of the total species diversity of the rainforest. *Photo Dennis Harding*

T asmania has more rainforest, as a proportion of its area, than any other State. Rainforest covers 765,000 hectares, or 11 per cent of the island.

The rainforest of Tasmania has many values. To scientists it is a source of knowledge. To wood workers of all kinds – cabinet makers, joiners, boat builders, crafts people – it provides timbers with special qualities. To tourists and bushwalkers it has a rare beauty. To the forest industries it is a large potential source of both sawlogs and pulpwood. To apiarists it is a source of a specially flavoured honey. To many native animals it is a place to live.

Tasmania's temperate rainforest is also a reminder of a world almost lost to us, containing within its living organisms information about our country's past. To enter the rainforest is to see the remnants of an ancient forest type once widespread in Australia but now reduced, outside Tasmania, to a few scattered patches.

This book has been prepared by the Working Group for Rainforest Conservation, established by the Tasmanian Government to recommend ways to protect the range of rainforest types. The book examines Tasmanian rainforest from many perspectives. Its purpose is both to provide general information about rainforest and to point out the many values and uses which need to be considered when making management decisions. This approach is founded on the belief that if such decisions are to meet the needs of our own and future generations, they must have wide public acceptance.

The Rainforest of Tasmania is intended primarily for the general reader. For this reason, common names for plants and animals have been used wherever possible in the text. Scientific names are listed in the glossary in *Appendix 1.*

WHAT·IS·TASMANIAN RAINFOREST?

◀ A moss-covered native plum.
Photo Jean Jarman

Tasmania contains Australia's largest tracts of cool temperate rainforest – a kind of rainforest very different from those of tropical and sub-tropical Australia. Unlike its northern counterparts, the trees of Tasmanian rainforest have no root buttresses. Leaves are generally much smaller. It has no palms, and lianes (climbing plants) are uncommon. In fact, Tasmanian rainforest has more in common with the beech forests of New Zealand and parts of South America than with Australia's sub-tropical and tropical rainforests.

▲
Winter adds a special character to rainforest at high altitudes.
Photo Dennis Harding

▶▶
King Billy pine and deciduous beech are two highly attractive rainforest species. *Photo Ted Mead*

▶
Celery top pines (olive green crowns) are one of nine dominant tree species which characterise rainforest in Tasmania.
Photo Dennis Harding

Many of the distinctive qualities of Tasmanian rainforest are well known: pictures of its moss-covered myrtles and dewy ferns have graced many a coffee table book or calendar. Yet a suitable definition of this unique forest type has been slow to evolve. One increasingly accepted approach is to define Tasmania's cool temperate rainforest in terms of the plants which characterise it.

Tasmanian rainforest is dominated by particular trees, or "canopy species", the most common of which is myrtle. Other characteristic rainforest trees are leatherwood and celery top pine, both of which grow on poorer soils; sassafras; Huon pine, which grows along river banks; and a number of sub-alpine trees including pencil and King Billy pines, deciduous beech and diselma.

Of the smaller rainforest plants, among the more prominent are manfern, native laurel, native plum, waratah, horizontal and pandani. A variety of mosses, lichens and fungi are also present.

All rainforest species have the ability to perpetuate themselves within forests dominated by one or more of the canopy species. They are able to regenerate in the absence of broad-scale disturbances, although some may depend on minor local disturbances such as windthrown trees or periodic flooding.

RELATED FOREST TYPES

Mixed forests: Vegetation with an understorey of rainforest species and an overstorey of eucalypts, which become sparse as the forest approaches maturity, is called mixed forest. Such forest is maintained by infrequent wildfires, at intervals of about 100 to 350 years, which allow the re-establishment of shade intolerant eucalypt seedlings. If fires are too infrequent, the eucalypts die out and the vegetation becomes rainforest.

Eucalypts are not rainforest species because they generally need fire to regenerate in natural conditions. However, for particular purposes forests containing some eucalypts may be classed as rainforest. For example, for forest management purposes a stand of rainforest species and eucalypts is con-sidered rainforest if the eucalypt crowns cover less than five per cent of the stand.

Blackwood swamp forests: These are similar to mixed forests, but in this case the dominant species are blackwood, teatree and paperbark, instead of eucalypts. Swamp forests are most extensive in north-western Tasmania, where they occupy slowly draining lowland flats. Rainforest trees such as myrtle, sassafras, leatherwood and celery top pine sometimes occur among the blackwoods, but they do not grow well in swampy land. Blackwood itself is not usually considered a rainforest species, because it also occurs commonly in other kinds of forests.

Blackwood and teatree regrowth, Welcome Swamp, north-western Tasmania. *Photo Robert Mesibov*
▶▶

▶
Mixed forest of stringybark and rainforest. *Photo Ken Felton*

EVOLUTION·OF·THE·RAINFOREST

◀

Rockfaces provide special habitats
for a variety of fern species. Some
species such as *Asplenium
trichomones* and *A. flabellifolium*
appear to be restricted to this
habitat. *Photo Dennis Harding*

EVOLUTION · OF · THE · RAINFOREST

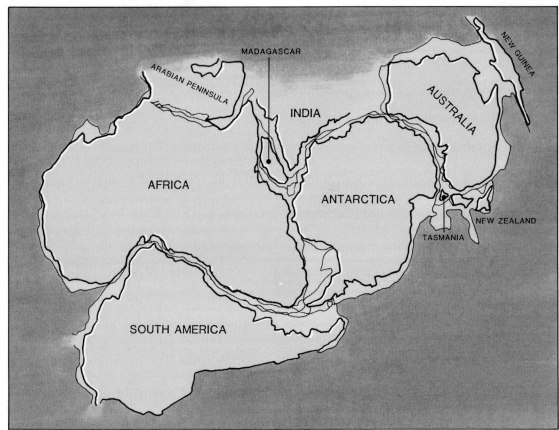

A ustralia is one of the most isolated of the world's large land masses. Its flora and fauna appear different from those of almost anywhere else on earth, and their origins have puzzled scientists since early European exploration. Some of the most important clues to the evolution of these unique life forms are to be found in the rainforests of Australia.

Tasmanian rainforest contains some of the most ancient species of Australia's flora. Most of its species are related to those found in the temperate forests of the Australian mainland, New Zealand and South America but fossil evidence indicates that the flora of Tasmanian rainforests also has links with plants that once grew in Antarctica. Such transcontinental connections help to support the now widely accepted theories of plate tectonics and continental drift.

Scientists working on the structure of the Earth's crust, with supporting evidence from fossils and living plants and animals, have developed the idea that the land masses we now know as Africa, South America, Antarctica, Australia and India, along with smaller land masses like New Zealand and Madagascar, were once all part of a southern supercontinent called Gondwana (*see Figure 1*). Each of these components of Gondwana was the visible part of what has been called a "plate". These plates (which still exist) move about slowly over many millions of years on the Earth's surface, some-times coming together, sometimes separating.

Geological evidence shows that around 130 million years ago Gondwana was beginning to break up. The first land masses to separate off were Africa, Madagascar and India, each "riding" on its own plate. New Zealand broke away from Australia about 85 million years ago, which left Australia, Antarctica and South America still connected.

The seas around this southern land mass were much warmer than they are now at similar latitudes, helping to produce a moist, mild climate which in turn supported a wide diversity of plant species. The early Gondwanan rainforests were a complex mixture of plants which today would be recognised as subtropical and temperate species. There were many different large trees, including emergent gymnosperms (conifers similar to Huon pine), and a dense understorey of shrubs, small trees, ferns (on the ground and growing on other plants), and lianes.

Evidence suggests that Australia, Antarctica and South America remained connected until around 50 million years ago. Subsequently, the Australian,

Antarctic and South American plates slowly drifted apart, and the Australian and South American plates moved gradually northward.

Patterns of ocean currents around the new island continent of Australia changed radically with the separation, and brought a very different climate. Generally drier conditions developed, with more extreme temperatures: in Tasmania, it became colder. Early Gondwanan plant species that failed to adapt to the new climate either died out or were confined to the wettest parts of the continent, particularly along the Great Dividing Range of eastern Australia. This range runs from north Queensland to Tasmania (which was last connected to the mainland of Australia as recently as 12,000 years ago).

Declining temperatures and rainfall dramatically changed the composition of Tasmania's rainforest. Descendants of many species which died out in Tasmania can be found today in the rainforests of Northern Australia and Papua New Guinea. New species have evolved from those that survived in Tasmania, the most obvious difference in the newer plants being smaller leaves. By the beginning of the Quaternary period (about two million years ago), the Tasmanian rainforest was dominated by microphyllous (small-leafed) plants.

Relatively recent changes in climate have profoundly altered the distribution of the Tasmanian flora. The last of a series of ice ages, or glaciations, ended in Tasmania about 12,000 years ago. During the last ice age the sea level was much lower than today, and Tasmania was joined to mainland Australia. Pollen evidence shows that the tree line was around present-day sea level in western Tasmania and about the 400 m level in the east. A warming climate caused ice to melt and sea levels to rise, and Tasmania again became an island.

Between 8000 and 5000 years ago the climate was warmer and wetter than today, which enabled rainforest to spread throughout much of the island. Since then, increasingly frequent droughts and frosts seem to have caused a reduction in the area of rainforest and an expansion of the eucalypt forests.

Some ancient remnants are important elements of today's Tasmanian rainforest. The smallest plants – the lichens and mosses – are among the oldest survivors, although relatively little is known about them. Ferns also are of ancient stock. Of the trees, the earliest to evolve include some of the native conifers, such as the genera *Lagarostrobos* (represented today by Huon pine), *Phyllocladus* (represented by celery top pine) and *Athrotaxis* (represented by pencil pine and King Billy pine). Huon pine is in the family Podocarpaceae, the first pollen records of which date back 135 million years. Of the flowering plants, *Nothofagus* (represented by myrtle and deciduous beech) is one of the most ancient genera, with pollen records dating back 85 million years.

▶

A dendrochronologist studies the growth rings on a Huon pine section. *Photo CSIRO*

Tree rings: a record of the past

Information on events of the past few thousand years can be obtained by studying growth rings in trees, a science called dendrochronology. The Tasmanian rainforest conifers are long lived and have very clear annual growth rings, making them particularly useful for such study. Huon pine reaches the greatest age: trees well over 2000 years old have been dated, placing the species

among the longest lived organisms on earth. Other species also have a long life span, including King Billy pine (about 1000 years) and celery top pine (about 800 years). This compares with the eucalypt's maximum life span of about 400 years.

Changing weather patterns bring variations in the width of tree rings, which can provide information about climatic patterns. A common pattern of ring width variation for each of the major conifers – King Billy, pencil, celery top and Huon pines – can be identified over the areas in which they occur. By matching overlapping growth ring patterns of both standing and fallen trees at a particular site, dendrochrono-logical records dating back centuries and even thousands of years can be constructed. Deciduous beech is par-ticularly sensitive to climate, but its value for climatic analysis is limited because it lives for only about 250 years.

▶
Pandani and deciduous beech. Although pandanis resemble certain palm species, they are dicotyledonous flowering plants in the heath family (Epacridaceae). They sometimes reach the size of small trees which can have unbranched stems over 10 metres tall. *Photo Rob Blakers*

3

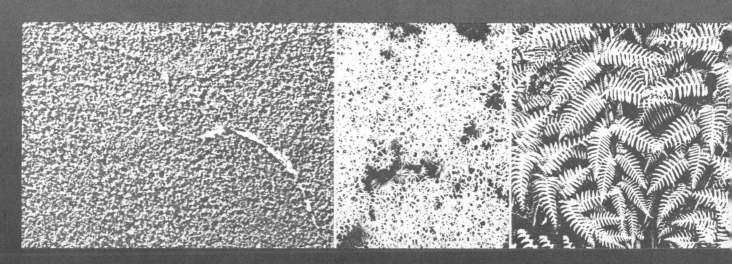

WHERE·IS·TASMANIA'S·RAINFOREST?
WHO·CONTROLS·IT?

WHERE·IS·TASMANIA'S·RAINFOREST?
WHO·CONTROLS·IT?

Rainforest occurs throughout western Tasmania, with some tracts in the north-eastern highlands and smaller patches elsewhere. The major occurrences are shown in *Figure 2*. Distribution is determined primarily by climate: rainforest occurs mostly where rainfall is high, usually well over 1200 millimetres a year, although there are many high rainfall places without rainforest. There are several explanations for these absences, such as the occurrence of past fires, or very low soil fertility, or, in the case of alpine areas, low temperatures. Small pockets of rainforest occur occasionally in drier parts of Tasmania, such as the hills on the east coast and Bruny Island, but these pockets are usually confined to wet gullies or places where moisture from clouds or mist supplements an otherwise inadequate rainfall.

The area of rainforest in Tasmania was estimated in 1984 to be 765,000 hectares. This represents about 20 per cent of Tasmania's forests and wood-

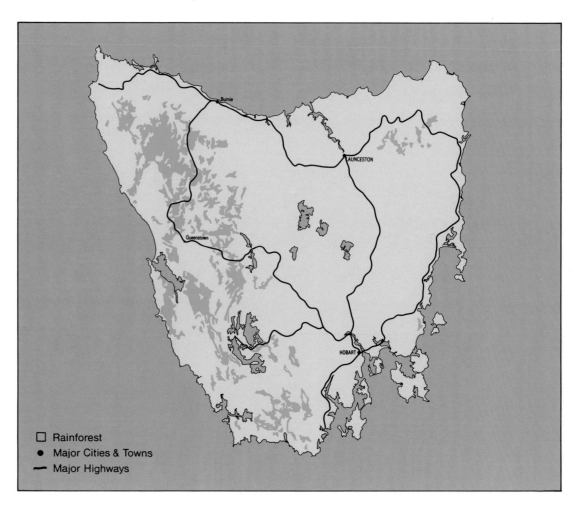

▶

Figure 2
Distribution of rainforest in Tasmania. *After Kirkpatrick and Dickinson, Vegetation Map of Tasmania, 1984*

☐ Rainforest
● Major Cities & Towns
— Major Highways

CONTROL OF TASMANIAN RAINFOREST

Responsible agency, Status	Percentage of rainforest	Proclamation/ revocation	Major uses	Production uses (eg timber, mining)
Department of Lands, Parks and Wildlife (DLPW)				
State Reserves, National Parks	26	Governor/ Parliament	Nature conservation, recreation	In absence of DLPW management plan to contrary, full legislative protection applies.
Conservation Areas under sole control of DLPW [1]	16	Governor/ Parliament	Nature conservation with controlled use of resources	Permitted in consultation with DLPW
Protected Areas	2	Minister for Lands, Parks and Wildlife	Nature conservation with controlled use of resources	Permitted
Unallocated Crown Land	26	Not applicable	Land bank for subsequent allocation	Permitted
Forestry Commission				
State Forest [2]	23	Governor/ Parliament	Wood production	Permitted
Forest Reserves [3]	1	Minister for Forests	Recreation, nature conservation	Timber harvesting prevented by management prescription; mining allowed
Hydro-Electric Commission				
Land associated with hydro-electric developments	2	Parliament	Catchment management	Permitted
Various owners [4]				
Private property	4	Not applicable	Wood production	Timber harvesting as prescribed by owners in accordance with Forest Practices Code; mining is allowed
TOTAL	100			

Footnotes – ([1]) Other areas, under joint control of DLPW and another land manager (eg State Forest within South-West Conservation Area), are ascribed to the other land owner. ([2]) Includes some Conservation Areas under joint management with DLPW, and in which wood production, taking account of conservation and recreation values, is permitted. ([3]) Areas of State Forest reserved for conservation or recreation. ([4]) The major owner is Associated Pulp and Paper Mills Ltd.

lands, and 11 per cent of the total land area. The estimate is based on the 1984 *Vegetation Map of Tasmania*, which includes, as rainforest, areas where dominant trees are rainforest species over eight metres tall.

The pre-European distribution of rainforest is poorly known. Much of the area climatically suited to rainforest supported other vegetation types because of the influence of fire, started either naturally (such as from lightning strikes) or by Aboriginal people. The advent of European settlement increased the frequency of fire in some areas (around Queenstown, for example), but in a few places such as the north-eastern highlands frequency has actually been reduced. A comparatively small area of rainforest has been cleared for farms and forest plantations. Such clearing has affected mixed forest much more than rainforest.

The tenure of Tasmania's rainforest, as indicated by the 1985 Land Map of Tasmania, is shown in the table on page 27.

This aerial photograph, scale 1:10,000, shows a section of the Vale River in north-western Tasmania. Tall eucalypts with large brown-green crowns can be seen on ridges. The river valley and its tributaries support rainforest which appears as a more uniform green. An area of sedgeland can be seen in the bottom left-hand corner.

Figure 3
This section of a forest-type map (Charter sheet, 1:25,000) was prepared from the aerial photograph above. The map has been enlarged to a scale of 1:10,000. Rainforest areas dominated by myrtle are shown as M, and eucalypt areas as E. Other vegetation types appearing on the map are Wm (mountain moor), S (scrub), T (secondary species) and ER (eucalypt regrowth). The numbers indicate height classes, and the lower-case letters indicate density classes.

☐ Rainforest
☐ Eucalypt & Mixed Forest
☐ Mountain moor & short scrub

Mapping the rainforest

Mapping the forests of an area as large as Tasmania is not an easy task. Large-scale forest-type maps, prepared from aerial photographs, cover most areas of State forest and some parts of unallocated Crown land. However, much less detailed information is available for the remaining Crown land, including National Parks. In 1984 Kirkpatrick and Dickinson produced a small-scale (1:500,000) vegetation map of Tasmania, based on information from forest-type maps, aerial photographs for previously unmapped areas, and ground surveys. The rainforest area estimate of 765,000 hectares included 56,000 hectares of forest recently burnt by wildfires and 53,000 hectares of rainforest/wet scrub mosaic.

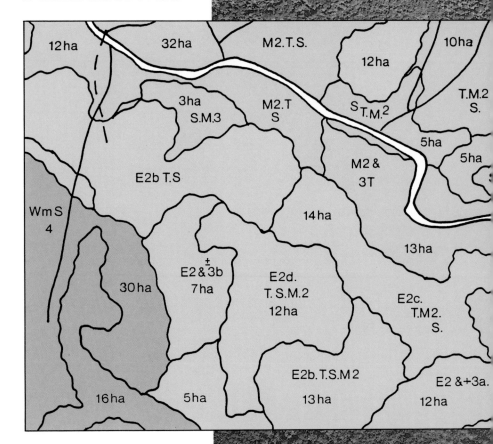

RAINFOREST·TYPES

◀ In autumn deciduous beech turns
a bright yellow before losing its
leaves. This species, the only
deciduous tree in Tasmania, is
more closely related to some of
the South American beeches than
to myrtle, the other beech found
in Tasmania. *Photo Ken Felton*

High altitude callidendrous rainforest occurs mainly in north-eastern Tasmania and on the Central Plateau. There are virtually no understorey shrubs. *Photo Grant Dixon*
▶▶

Callidendrous sassafras-musk rainforest occurs as relic rainforest stands in fire protected gullies in eastern Tasmania. *Photo Jean Jarman*
▼

Tasmanian rainforest can be divided into four basic structural **types**: callidendrous, thamnic, implicate and open montane. The latter three are endemic (found only in Tasmania). Callidendrous rainforest also occurs in Victoria, but is better developed in Tasmania.

These main types can be further subdivided into 39 plant **communities**, each community being a naturally recurring group of different plants inhabiting a common environment. Frequent intermixing between these communities results in continuous variations within the rainforest vegetation.

Primary communities are identified according to characteristic understorey species such as musk, horizontal, native laurel, native plum and white waratah. Within each primary community there are further subdivisions based on the dominant tree species. A list of rainforest communities is shown in *Appendix III*.

Callidendrous rainforest gives a park-like impression, with trees from about 25 to 40 metres high, mostly myrtle with some sassafras, and an open understorey of only a few inconspicuous shrubs and, sometimes, manferns. Five different callidendrous communities have been recognised.

Thamnic rainforest has trees of a height similar to those of callidendrous forest, but is more shrubby below. Myrtle, leatherwood, celery top pine and sassafras are the most common canopy species. Researchers have discerned 16 different thamnic rainforest communities.

Implicate rainforest has shorter trees, usually below 20 metres, with a dense shrub understorey. The trees and shrubs form a continuous, tangled network of twisted stems and low branches. There are many different species present in this type of rainforest. Eight different implicate rainforest communities have been distinguished.

Open montane rainforest, as its name indicates, is found only in high country. The dominant trees, pencil pines, are short and widely spaced, amid a dense scrub understorey. Four communities have been identified.

Another recognisable type is **gallery rainforest**, but this is restricted to margins of streams and lakes and is often only a few metres wide. Only one gallery rainforest community has been described.

▲

Callidendrous fern rainforest of myrtle, manfern and mother shield fern. This community is common on fertile soils in north-western and north-eastern Tasmania. *Photo Robert Shepherd*

▲
Thamnic horizontal rainforest
often contains widely spaced
myrtle and leatherwood trees
amidst thick horizontal shrubbery.
The community is widespread in
western and south-western
Tasmania and also extends into
the North-West. It often occurs
near creeks. *Photo Jean Jarman*

Five intermediate rainforest communities, not fitting precisely into any
of the main types, have also been
reported.

The proportion of Tasmanian
endemic plants is relatively low in callidendrous rainforests, but increases in
thamnic, implicate and open montane
forests. The number of flowering plant
and conifer species follows a similar

trend, but fern species are usually found
in greater numbers in callidendrous
forests than in the other groups.

The boundary between callidendrous rainforest and the two other major
types (thamnic and implicate) is more
or less a diagonal line across the State
from north-west to south-east. The
most extensive callidendrous forests
occur in the North-West, with patches

in eastern, south-eastern and central Tasmania. Thamnic and implicate rainforests are found mostly in the south-west and west. The map *(Figure 4)* shows the broad regional division of the rainforest types in Tasmania.

Soil fertility appears to be important in determining the type of rainforest in any particular place. Callidendrous rainforests are generally found on more fertile soils, such as those derived from basalt. Thamnic rainforests tend to occur on soils of medium to low fertility, while implicate forests are often found on very poor soils. Altitude is important in determining the distribution of open montane forest, while another factor may be rock type.

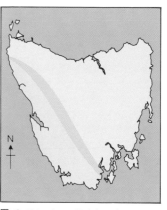

☐ Callidendrous Rainforest
☐ Thamnic & Implicate Rainforest

▲

Figure 4
Broad regional division of rainforest types (after Jarman *et al*, 1984)

◄

Flowering leatherwood in **Thamnic laurel rainforest**. This community is dominated by myrtle and leatherwood over a shrubby understorey which includes native laurel and native plum. It is common in southern and south-western Tasmania on well-drained sites. *Photo Ken Felton*

◄◄

Thamnic Archeria rainforest with Huon pine. This community is dominated by Huon pine (yellow-green crowns) and myrtle (olive-green crowns). *Archeria eriocarpa* is the main species in the scattered shrub layer. The community occurs on several south-western rivers such as the Davey (pictured), Wanderer and Jane. *Photo Steve Harris*

Thamnic Trochocarpa gunnii – pandani rainforest is dominated by King Billy pine, with an understorey mostly of *Trochocarpa gunnii* and pandanis. The community occurs on mountain slopes of south-western Tasmania above 700 m.
Photo Jean Jarman

Implicate deciduous beech forest is often less than 10 m high, and dominated by King Billy pine (bright green crowns). Diselma is sometimes present (conical dark green crowns) and the understorey is mostly deciduous beech (appearing as grey leafless shrubs in the photograph). The community is uncommon and confined to high altitudes in the west and south-west. *Photo Jean Jarman*

▶

Implicate Trochocarpa climbing heath rainforest has a broken canopy of myrtle, leatherwood and celery top pine. In the tangled uneven understorey, *Trochocarpa gunnii* is the most common species. Climbing heath is prolific, forming dense tangles on fallen logs and the trunks and low branches of trees. The community occurs occasionally in south-western Tasmania. *Photo Jean Jarman*

Montane pencil pine forest over coniferous heath occurs occasionally on the Central Plateau. The understorey species include conifers such as diselma, *Microstrobos niphophilus* and *Podocarpus lawrencii*.
Photo Jean Jarman

Montane pencil pine forest over grassland has trees up to 15m tall which are often multi-stemmed. The community is park-like, with a closely grazed, grassy understorey.
Photo Robert Shepherd

43

Gallery rainforest occurs as a narrow band between the water's edge of some major rivers and the adjoining forest. It is subject to frequent flooding and often contains poorly formed trees of myrtle, Huon pine and leatherwood amidst a shrubbery of *Leptospermum riparium*. Examples of this community are found on the Gordon, Franklin, Huon, Picton and Pieman Rivers. *Photo Jean Jarman*

The following illustrations show the main species and the occurrence of typical rainforest communities within each rainforest type. Species listed in brackets are those which are only sometimes present.

Main Species:

myrtle, sassafras (blackwood, wallaby wood)
manferns
ferns, mosses and liverworts

Occurrence:

fertile soils, lowland areas

F. DUNCAN 1987

Main Species:

myrtle, woolly teatree (sassafras, celery top pine)
waratah, mountain pepper

Main Species:

sassafras (myrtle, *Eucalyptus regnans*, woolly teatree)
manferns, musk
ferns

Occurrence:

fertile soils, upland areas

Occurrence:

eastern Tasmania; scattered in gullies and other sites with very high moisture availability

Main Species:

myrtle, leatherwood celery top pine
(sassafras, Huon pine)
horizontal
mosses, liverworts (ferns)

Occurrence:

lowlands of west and southwest, often
associated with rivers

Main Species:

Leptospermum riparium
(*Epacris mucronulata*,
leatherwood, Huon pine, myrtle,
Acradenia)
bryophytes, ferns, herbs

Occurrence:

banks of larger rivers in western
Tasmania

F. DUNCAN 1987

Main Species:

myrtle, leatherwood, celery top pine
(sassafras)
Trochocarpa spp., *Archeria*
bryophytes, ferns

Main Species:

King Billy pine
(myrtle, leatherwood, celery top pine)
pandani, dwarf leatherwood (horizontal, deciduous
beech, *Archeria*, *Trochocarpa*)
bryophytes (herbs)

Occurrence:

lowlands and uplands

Occurrence:

mountain slopes and highlands

49

Main Species:

celery top pine, myrtle, leatherwood,
(Huon pine, sassafras, paperbark, teatree)
horizontal, native laurel, native plum, white
waratah
(*Archeria*, *Trochocarpa*, climbing heath,
cutting grass)

Main Species:

woolly teatree, celery top pine,
myrtle (sassafras, leatherwood)
horizontal, native laurel, native plum
(*Trochocarpa*, *Archeria*, cutting grass)

Occurrence:

lowland

Occurrence:

poorly drained lowland sites

F. DUNCAN 1987

Main Species:

King Billy pine, myrtle, leatherwood,
celery top pine (teatree)
white waratah, pandani (horizontal,
native laurel, native plum, scoparia,
climbing heath)

Main Species:

King Billy pine, celery top pine, deciduous beech,
(myrtle, leatherwood)
diselma (pandani, scoparia)

Occurrence:

high altitude (above 500m)

Occurrence:

high altitude (above 800m)

51

Main Species:

pencil pine
Poa spp., *Danthonia spp.*

Occurrence:

fine soils on highland areas
e.g. Walls of Jerusalem

Main Species:

pencil pine
diselma, *Microcachrys, Microstrobos*
scoparia, O*ites, Leptospermum rupestre*

Occurrence:

rocky sites in highland areas,
e.g. widespread on Central Plateau

F. DUNCAN 1987

pencil pine, deciduous beech
pandani

boulderfields and rocky sites in highland areas
e.g. Mt Field, Labyrinth

5

ANIMALS·OF·THE·RAINFOREST

The eastern pygmy possum is found in south-eastern Australia, but is not common. Its Tasmanian habitat is mainly rainforest areas, although it does occur elsewhere. The animal is very small, weighing only about 40 grams. During cold periods they go into a state of torpor to conserve energy, and live off stored fat in the thickened base of the tail.
Photo Annie Wapstra

▶▶

Tasmanian devils are found over a range of vegetation types including rainforest. They are born in litters of two or three and reach maturity after their second year.
Photo Dave Watts

▼

The rainforests of Tasmania are home to many of the island's unique species of animals. Tasmania's isolation over many thousands of years has allowed species to survive free from the competition of animals from elsewhere. Furthermore, its climate is cooler, wetter and more temperate than that of mainland Australia. The fauna unique to Tasmania, or which has its stronghold on the island, is therefore most commonly found in the wetter forests, both eucalypt forest and rainforest. Some of the primitive invertebrate fauna of Tasmania appears to have a close affinity with species found in fossil form in Antarctica, with which Australia was once linked in the ancient supercontinent, Gondwana.

Mammals

Twenty-two mammal species have been found in Tasmanian rainforest, about two-thirds of the total for the State. None of these is found only in rainforest, and 14 of them occur more commonly in other habitats. Only the endemic long-tailed mouse makes its home primarily in rainforest. No rainforest mammal is considered an endangered species in Tasmania.

Introduced mammals are rarely found in rainforest. Only the house mouse and the feral cat have been recorded, but neither is widespread. Mammals that occur in rainforests of Tasmania can be divided into six classes according to feeding habits:

- **Carnivores** – Tasmanian devil, spotted-tailed quoll or tiger cat
- **Insectivores** (or insect-eating mammals) – dusky antechinus or marsupial mouse, echidna
- **Bats** – lesser long-eared bat, little forest bat, chocolate bat
- **Tree herbivores** – ringtail possum
- **Ground herbivores** – Tasmanian pademelon or rufous wallaby
- **Rodents** – swamp rat, long-tailed mouse

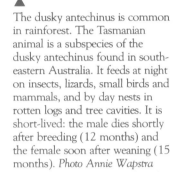

The dusky antechinus is common in rainforest. The Tasmanian animal is a subspecies of the dusky antechinus found in south-eastern Australia. It feeds at night on insects, lizards, small birds and mammals, and by day nests in rotten logs and tree cavities. It is short-lived: the male dies shortly after breeding (12 months) and the female soon after weaning (15 months). *Photo Annie Wapstra*

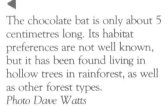

The chocolate bat is only about 5 centimetres long. Its habitat preferences are not well known, but it has been found living in hollow trees in rainforest, as well as other forest types.
Photo Dave Watts

The rufous wallaby, or pademelon, is widespread in Tasmania although its preferred habitat is rainforest, wet eucalypt forest and teatree scrub.
Photo Annie Wapstra

The spotted-tailed quoll, or tiger cat, is a marsupial found in rainforest and wet eucalypt forest in Tasmania, and on the eastern Australian mainland. It has a shallow pouch and produces litters of six. It feeds mostly on carrion, small mammals and birds.
Photo Annie Wapstra

The olive whistler is common in Tasmanian rainforest, as well as other wet forest and coastal woodlands dominated by teatree. It has a distinctive, musical "whee-too" whistle. *Photo Dave Watts*

▶▶
The southern boobook owl nests in hollows in both living and dead trees in rainforests, eucalypt forests and woodlands. Unlike other owl species, the boobook feeds mostly on insects rather than small birds and mammals. *Photo Dave Watts*

Birds

Twenty-one species – all native – are regular rainforest inhabitants. All are fairly common, and no bird species is found only in Tasmanian rainforest.

The birds of the rainforest can be divided into 10 groups according to their feeding preferences.

- **Bark-searching insectivores** – yellow-tailed black cockatoo, yellow-throated honeyeater, crescent honey-eater, grey shrike thrush

- **Seed-eating parrots** – green rosella
- **Understorey insectivores** – pink robin, grey fantail, scrubtit, olive whistler, Tasmanian thornbill
- **Nectarivores** – eastern spinebill
- **Foliage insectivores** – golden whistler, silvereye
- **Trunk-feeding insectivores** – shining bronze cuckoo
- **Ground-feeding omnivores** – black currawong, forest raven

- **Ground feeders** – brush bronze-wing, Whites thrush
- **Litter fossickers** – white-browed scrubwren
- **Carnivores** – grey goshawk, southern boobook

Other bird species can be found near the edges of rainforest, including the white-breasted sea eagle, the collared sparrowhawk and the masked owl.

The grey goshawk is widespread throughout eastern Australia and in New Guinea, although it occurs at low population densities. In Tasmania it frequents rainforest areas. The large female hunts in the forest canopy, preying on such birds as herons, currawongs and parrots. The pure white phase is predominant in Tasmania.
Photo Dave Watts

◄◄▲
Green rosellas, endemic to Tasmania, are common in many parts of the island. They live primarily in eucalypt forests, but their frequent visits to rainforest areas provide a welcome splash of colour. *Photo Dave Watts*

◄▲
The masked owl is rarely seen in mainland Australia, but is more common in Tasmanian forests, including rainforest.
Photo Dave Watts

The endemic yellow-throated honeyeater is found in virtually all vegetation types, from rainforest to domestic gardens.
Photo Dave Watts

◄▲
Black currawongs occur in rainforest, mixed forest and wet eucalypt forest. They are readily seen at picnic sites especially when there is food about.
Photo Peter Walton

61

The Tasmanian tree frog is a strikingly handsome species found in rainforest, sedgelands and alpine moors. It is widespread in western Tasmania.
Photo Dave Watts
◀

A tiger snake finds a comfortable resting place on a mossy log in implicate rainforest.
Photo Jean Jarman
▼▶

The brown tree frog is smaller than the Tasmanian tree frog. It has a wide distribution and can be found throughout Tasmania near both permanent and temporary water. It is found widely in rainforest. *Photo Dave Watts*
◀◀◀

◀◀
Oak skinks are found in a variety of habitats, including rocky areas in rainforest. These nocturnal lizards measure about 130 millimetres from snout to vent, and can be found during the day in leaf litter or under fallen logs.
Photo Dave Watts

◀
The endemic Tasmanian froglet is a relatively inconspicuous species. It is widespread in the north and west and highlands.
Photo Dave Watts

Reptiles

Six species of reptiles are found in Tasmanian rainforest, but none is confined to it.

Among the most commonly encountered are the tiger snake and a species of brown skink. The white-lipped whip snake and the oak skink are also quite common. Other rainforest species, found in more open or rocky areas, are the blotched blue-tongued lizard and two skink species endemic to Tasmania, *Leiolopisma pretiosum* and *L. ocellatum*.

Amphibians

The limited amount of research so far on Tasmanian rainforest amphibia shows that there are at least four rainforest species, though none is confined to rainforest.

The brown tree frog is most widespread, living in closed forest (forest with more than 70 per cent cover) as well as in more open areas. The Tasmanian tree frog occurs in similar habitats but is restricted to western Tasmania. The common froglet and the related endemic Tasmanian froglet also occur in rainforest, although the latter is not found under closed canopies.

Anoglypta launcestonensis is a large land snail endemic to the rainforest of the north-eastern highlands. The snail is 25 to 35 mm long, and rarely seen alive. It makes its home in cavities in rotten logs, or in deep, wet leaf litter. *Photo Rod Smith*

Macleay's swallowtail is probably Tasmania's most attractive butterfly. The caterpillars feed on sassafras leaves while adults feed on nectar from blossom of leatherwood, teatree and other flowers. *Photo John Voss*

Yabby mounds, a common sight in rainforest, are the work of several species of burrowing freshwater crayfish. Yabbies excavate long and complicated burrow systems, part of which fill with water. They feed on dead plant material in the flooded burrows. *Photo Jean Jarman*

Invertebrates (animals without backbones)

Invertebrates include a huge number of diverse animals such as insects, spiders, snails, crayfish, leeches and earthworms. It has been estimated that invertebrate species found in Tasmania may number more than 30,000, a high proportion of which are confined to the State. Endemic invertebrates are often associated with endemic plants, which suggests that Tasmania's rainforest and alpine areas, rich in unique flora, have the highest proportion of endemic invertebrate species.

There is much to be learned about the invertebrate animals of Tasmanian rainforest, and in many of the more remote places little collecting has been done. Already, however, it appears that Tasmanian rainforest contains some of the most ancient and primitive representatives of a number of invertebrate groups.

The conditions under a closed rainforest canopy – dark, sheltered, moist – are an attractive environment to many species which cannot survive under dry, sunny conditions. Rotting logs are one specialised micro-habitat, colonised by numerous species. Although poorly studied, another micro-habitat which is likely to support a special invertebrate fauna is the litter underneath endemic rainforest conifers such as Huon, King Billy and celery top pines.

▶

Ooperipatus insignis is a member of a small group of animals which have worm-like bodies and many unjointed legs. This group, known as the Onychophera (walking worms) is fascinating to biologists because it is intermediate between the Annelids (such as earthworms and leeches) and the Arthropods (including spiders, insects and crustaceans). *O. insignis* is found under rotting logs and other similar places in wet forests of Tasmania, as well as mainland Australia. It is a predator with an unusual method of capturing its prey. It fires a thin stream of "superglue" with pinpoint accuracy from two organs on the top of its head. It then injects digestive juices into its immobile victim, sucking it dry.
Photo K. Lim

THE·ECOLOGY·OF·THE·RAINFOREST

◀
Old myrtle trees are sometimes
festooned with an array of moss
and lichen species.
Photo Grant Dixon

THE·ECOLOGY·OF·THE·RAINFOREST

A rainforest is more than simply an accumulation of organisms. It needs to be seen in terms of the relationships between its plants and animals and their physical environment; in other words, as an ecosystem. Biologists still have much to learn about rainforest ecology, but they are beginning to understand principles of regeneration of dominant forest trees, nutrient cycling, the effects of fire and the role of damaging and disease-causing organisms.

Natural regeneration of dominant trees

Though the rainforest is self-perpetuating, there is competition between species to maintain their place in the forest.

Each tree species has its own regeneration strategy. Myrtle trees, for example, seed prolifically at roughly three-year intervals, with very little seed produced in intervening years. After heavy seedfalls, very large numbers of newly germinated myrtle seedlings can be found on the forest floor. Where they occur on a suitable seedbed and have enough light, such as under canopy gaps created by storm damage or dying trees, they become established and grow. Heavily shaded seedlings usually die out within a couple of seasons. Leatherwoods produce seed annually and regenerate in a manner similar to that of myrtle. Sassafras is able to grow in lower light than any other dominant rainforest species, but its seedlings are highly susceptible to drought and browsing by animals. Successful seedling regeneration is usually confined to protected sites such as high on the trunks of manferns. Sassafras trees commonly replace themselves by basal sprouts: when a tree crown dies from old age a new stem from the same rootstock takes its place.

The regeneration mechanisms of the main rainforest conifers, Huon pine, King Billy pine and celery top pine, are not well understood. The latter two appear to regenerate intermittently from seed, presumably in response to some relatively rare climatic or environmental event. However, King Billy pine can regenerate more or less continuously when grown in forests with a high proportion of deciduous beech. This is probably because more light reaches the ground in these forests than under evergreen trees. Huon pine commonly regenerates vegetatively from fallen stems which produce new upright shoots along their length, and possibly also from small branchlets broken from tree crowns. Seedling regeneration of Huon pine does occur, but seems less common than vegetative reproduction.

Blackwood is often abundant in

▲
Pencil pines and deciduous beech. Pencil pine is usually the sole tree species in open montane rainforests. *Photo Grant Dixon*

▶▶
Sassafras trees often replace a dying or broken stem with a new one from the same root system. This sassafras tree has five stems of various sizes, including a young sapling. While individual stems often live only about 200 years, the root systems can be very much older. *Photo John Hickey*

recently burnt rainforest. Although the tree is relatively short-lived, usually less than 200 years, its seeds are very hardy, and can be stored in the soil for decades, perhaps centuries. The seed will germinate in massive amounts following a fire. At other times, blackwood regeneration in rainforest is largely confined to locally disturbed sites such as river banks and the root mounds formed by windthrown trees.

Nutrient cycling

Like all forests, rainforests derive their nutrients from several sources, including the soil (weathered rock), the atmosphere (as gases fixed by microorganisms) and salts brought in by rain. These nutrients are cycled by the plants: taken up by roots, used for growth and returned to the soil by leaf and branch falls. Through grazing, herbivorous animals are able to capture nutrients from the plants, in turn providing nutrients for carnivores. Both plant and animal debris or litter is decomposed by soil microorganisms such as fungi and bacteria until it is in a form which is again available to plants. Nutrients are removed from the system by the leaching effect of water and through gases given off by plants.

An interesting facet of nutrient cycling in Tasmanian rainforests is the marked difference in depth between the litter layer in callidendrous rainforests and that in thamnic and implicate forests. In callidendrous rainforests there is usually only a few centimetres of leaf litter above the mineral soil, but thamnic and implicate forests often have very deep layers which become compressed to form fibrous peat or organic soils which can be up to a metre thick. It seems that litter decomposes at a much faster rate in callidendrous rainforest than in the other two types.

▲
Female cones of Huon pine. Male and female cones are borne on separate trees. The female cones, only 3mm long, hang as though dripping from the smaller branchlets. *Photo Trevor Bird*

▶
Huon pine propagules (seeds and broken branchlets) are primarily dispersed by water along rivers. Regeneration is usually abundant along river banks. However, in undisturbed stands away from rivers seedling regeneration is a less frequent event.
Photo Grant Dixon

A Huon pine seedling less than a year old, still bearing its cotyledons. *Photo John Pedley*
▼

▲

Myrtle seedlings can grow quite quickly – up to about 30 cm a year – where there is a gap in the canopy and where their roots are well established in mineral soil.
Photo Andrew Blakesley

◄

King Billy pine cones contain dozens of seeds which resemble toasted oats. The trees produce cones about once every five or six years, and these are very conspicuous in a heavy coning year. The seed is viable for only a few months after it is shed.
Photo Jean Jarman

Celery top pine seedlings have needle-like leaves until about 10 cm tall. Then they produce their characteristic "leaves" (actually flattened stems known as cladodes) which give the species its common name.
Photo Jean Jarman

▼

Although fungi are plants they contain no chlorophyll, which means they cannot produce their own food through photosynthesis. Instead they survive by decomposing other organic material, both living and dead. The rainforest supports a wide variety of fungi, many of them quite spectacular. Autumn is the best time to see them.

▶

Heterobasidion hemitephrum is a bracket fungus commonly associated with dead and dying myrtle trees. It causes a white rot of the heartwood. The horizontal layers on the bracket represent annual growth rings.
Photo Jean Jarman

Another bracket fungus is *Tyromyces pulcherrimus*, which occurs on *Nothofagus* species in Tasmania, Victoria and New Zealand. *Photo Jean Jarman*
▼

Large myrtle trees. Myrtle is the tallest rainforest species, and can be up to 50 metres tall on the most favourable sites.
Photo Ted Mead

▶

78

The role of fire

Fire has had a profound influence in determining forest types in Tasmania. Vegetation patterns can be linked with fire frequency, and while there are also other factors, a general rule applying to the wetter parts of the island is that the less frequent the fire, the greater the chance that rainforest will develop.

In these wetter regions, areas where fires occur very frequently tend to support such vegetation as grasslands, sedgelands and heaths. Most tree species are eliminated because they are not allowed enough time to reach seeding age, which for many species is about 20 years.

◄

This delicate agaric or gilled fungus, *Coprinus disseminatus*, commonly occurs on the soil, litter and decaying wood beneath rainforest. The fungus has a worldwide distribution.
Photo Nick Mooney

"Myrtle oranges" are the fruiting bodies of the fungus *Cyttaria gunnii*, which causes branch galls on myrtle trees. *Cyttaria* species occur on *Nothofagus* in Australia, New Zealand and Chile.
Photo Ken Felton
▼

Where fires occur less often but within intervals of around 100 years, and where the soil is fertile enough, the most likely vegetation is a wet sclerophyll forest: eucalypts with an understorey of broad-leaved shrubs such as native pear, blanket leaf and lancewood. Wet sclerophyll species are generally shade-intolerant, rarely being able to regenerate under a forest canopy, but where wild-fires have removed the shade they can colonise rapidly. The seeds of some wet sclerophyll species can remain viable in the soil for many decades, while the seeds of others are adapted for transport by wind over long distances. Eucalypt seed is formed in thick, woody capsules, and can survive even when a fire has destroyed the parent tree. It is not well adapted for wind dispersal, so most seedlings occur within a radius roughly equivalent to the height of the parent tree.

Longer intervals between fires allow time for rainforest species to increase in number from the occasional rainforest seedlings and coppice shoots resulting from the last fire. After two or three centuries of virtually continuous regeneration by rainforest species, a dense understorey develops. After about 400 years, the last of the non-rainforest species, including eucalypts, have died out, leaving rainforest.

There are exceptions to this process. For example, when fires occur in large patches of rainforest well removed from non-rainforest seed sources, the vegetation can often regenerate back to rainforest without passing through the intermediate stages of wet sclerophyll and mixed forest. The resulting regrowth is even-aged and often very dense, and commonly referred to as a pole stand. After about 200 years, these pole stands begin to break up as some trees die and new ones regenerate in the gaps they leave. They gradually assume the more familiar multi-aged appearance of most rainforest.

The threat from fire

Most rainforest species are easily killed by fire. Some, including deciduous beech and the conifers Huon pine, King Billy pine and pencil pine, do not seem to have any means of surviving severe fire. Several other rainforest species, including myrtle, sassafras and leather-wood, are less fire-sensitive, having some ability to produce shoots or grow from

Celery top pine seedling regeneration and native plum coppice regeneration 10 years after a fire in rainforest at the Sawback Range. Celery top pine is better able to regenerate after fire than the other rainforest conifers. Some of the seed for regeneration may come from the crowns of burnt trees but most is stored in the soil or brought in by birds. *Photo Frank Podger*
▶

A lightning strike was responsible for this fire which killed a large stand of King Billy pine on Algonkian Mountain. There is often little or no pine regeneration after such fires. *Photo Ken Felton*
◀▼

Coppice shoots on a leatherwood tree burnt in the 1982 Savage River fire. Many trees did not resprout, but there were enough for a continuing seed supply as long as there are no subsequent fires in the next few decades. *Photo John Hickey*
▼

seed after fire. It would usually take a number of wildfires over a few decades to eliminate such species from a site. Unfortunately, burnt rainforest is often invaded by an abundance of non-rain-forest species which, because they are usually more flammable than rainforest plants, increase the risk of further fires.

Wildfires, most of them lit by people, are the most serious threat to conservation of rainforest in Tasmania. Large wildfires do occur in rainforest under extreme conditions: this was clearly demonstrated by a devastating fire which started near Savage River in 1982 and burnt more than 10,000 hectares of rainforest. Since 1950 about eight percent of Tasmania's rainforest has been burnt, and while it is unlikely that rainforest will be eliminated through fire, some special areas have already been destroyed and may never recover. Much of the pencil pine forests of the Central Plateau which were burnt in 1961 still show no sign of regeneration. On King Island, naturally occurring celery top pine and sassafras have been eliminated since European settlement as a result of fire and clearing.

Pests and diseases

Death is an integral part of the rainforest ecosystem, but there are some organisms which are capable of causing enough damage to alter the equilibrium between growth and decay.

Myrtle wilt is a serious disease which kills myrtles. It is caused by a fungus, *Chalara australis*, which appears to be spread as wind-borne spores throughout the forest. The fungus can enter the tree through wounds such as

◄

Rainforest and mixed forest burnt by the Savage River fire. Black patches indicate areas burnt by crown fires while brown areas were burnt by ground fires. Unburnt rainforest formed occasional islands and narrow bands along many of the creeks and rivers. *Photo John Hickey*

broken branches. While it occurs in undisturbed areas of forest, its local effects may be increased by human activity. For example, myrtle wilt can be seen along road edges where trees have been damaged by road construction.

Myrtle trees are also highly susceptible to mass infestation by a small beetle known as the mountain pinhole borer, which attacks living myrtles by boring tiny holes through the sapwood. The beetle usually does not kill the host tree, but it may weaken it and allow access to lethal fungi, such as *Chalara*. The beetle also attacks other rainforest trees and eucalypts, but to a much smaller extent than myrtle.

A second fungus, *Phytophthora cinnamomi*, causes root rot in some rainforest plants, usually followed by death. Generally, soil temperatures are too low under a closed rainforest canopy for the fungus to be destructive, but it can affect more open rainforest and adjacent heath and scrub. The fungus may also be active in areas where the canopy has been damaged – by fire, for example.

While *Chalara australis* and the mountain pinhole borer are believed to be native to Tasmania, *Phytophthora cinnamomi* is an introduced species.

▲
This pencil pine forest on the Central Plateau was destroyed by an extensive wildfire in 1961 known to have been deliberately lit. *Photo Rob Blakers*

▶

Sections of myrtle logs from trees killed by myrtle wilt show extensive staining of the sapwood by the fungus *Chalara australis.* *Photo Humphrey Elliott*

This oblique aerial photograph of undisturbed rainforest in the King River valley shows the prevalence of myrtle wilt. Trees with brown foliage are recently dead, while the grey trees are those which have been killed within about the past three years. *Photo Jean Jarman*

▼

7

COMMERCIAL · USES

◄

This unique blackwood dining
setting is the work of Helmut
Lueckenhausen. Helmut's work is
exhibited in the Australian
National Gallery in Canberra, as
well as in four State collections.
Photo Peter Jeffs

7 COMMERCIAL·USES

Tasmania's rainforests and the land on which they stand have considerable commercial value. Some commercial uses, such as timber production, tourism and leatherwood honey production, depend on the rainforest itself. Others involve alternative uses of rainforested land, including mining, forest plantations, hydro-electric developments and agriculture. These latter uses, however, need to be carefully planned and managed to avoid damage to adjacent rainforest through fire, erosion, weed infestation and pollution.

Timber from rainforest

Past and present: The high value and unique qualities of Tasmanian rainforest timbers have long been recognised. Huon pine, closely grained, soft and extremely durable, was the first to be commercially exploited, particularly for shipbuilding and furniture making. As early as 1815 major river valleys of western Tasmania were explored for this species, and the notorious convict settlement in Macquarie Harbour (1822-1833) was founded largely to exploit the pine resources of the lower Gordon and King River valleys. Huon pine logs have the added advantage of floating while green, which enables them to be transported on water.

Huon pine has remained the most prized rainforest timber, but development of the western Tasmanian mining industry late in the 19th century brought increased use of two other durable rainforest conifers – King Billy pine and celery top pine. King Billy pine, now only available from salvage logging, is still used in joinery and boat construction. It can be carved easily, but is not suited to turning. Celery top pine is commonly used in boat building, as cladding for houses and as decking timber.

Of the hardwoods, myrtle is only moderately durable, but is excellent for cabinet making and turning, and has also been used in flooring and wood panelling. Unfortunately, myrtle trees are very susceptible to a variety of stem-rotting fungi, which results in a high proportion of defective timber. The soundest myrtle is found on deep, fertile soils such as those derived from basalt rock.

Sassafras timber once had a wide range of uses, including the manufacture of clothes pegs, but in this broader commercial role it has since been replaced by radiata pine. Some sassafras has a very dark heartwood, and its timber is referred to as "black heart sassafras". The dark staining, probably the initial stages of decay, is caused by

▲

This four poster Huon pine bed was made in Hobart in the mid-1800s. From the collection of Colin Self, Hobart.
Photo supplied by Colin Self

▶▶

Piners camp sheltering under Huon pine on the Lower Gordon River in 1908. *Photo J.W. Beattie*

A gentleman's Huon pine chest of drawers with picture-frame hat drawer in centre, made in Tasmania about 1870. The oil in Huon pine helps to repel insects which attack clothing. From the De Witt Collection, Hobart.
Photo Geoff Tyson

This bread box features striking use of black heart sassafras. Courtesy Lifestyle Furniture, Hobart.
Photo Uffe Schulze
▼▶

Celery top pine drawer cabinet, 450 x 300 x 250 mm, made by Peter Walker while a wood design student at the School of Art, University of Tasmania.
Photo Uffe Schulze
▼

water-borne bacteria which gain access through broken crowns and branches. Black heart sassafras has found favour among wood turners and furniture makers for its distinctive colour and grain.

Most blackwood timber is used for furniture and wall panelling and in veneer production. Although much of the former blackwood swamp land in north-western Tasmania has now been drained and cleared for agriculture, about 8000 hectares have been set aside for timber production.

In the mid-1980s, the annual cut of non-eucalypt native species for saw-logs – including blackwood and silver wattle – was about 27,000 cubic metres a year. This represents about four per cent of the annual Tasmanian sawlog production from all Crown forests. Since 1982 the logging of large rain-forested areas has been suspended to allow investigation of both conservation needs and techniques for regeneration. Currently the demand for rainforest species sawlogs is met mainly from harvesting in mixed forest.

Average annual sawlog cut of non-eucalypt native species for the period 1981-82 to 1985-86

Species	Sawlogs (m³/year)	Major source
blackwood	12,500	blackwood swamps, mixed forest
celery top pine	6,500	mixed forest
myrtle	5,000	mixed forest
Huon pine	500	rainforest*
King Billy pine	200	rainforest*
Other native species (sassafras, leatherwood, silver wattle)	1,800	mixed forest, wet sclerophyll forest

* Most of this total was salvaged from valleys to be flooded for generation of hydro-electricity.

Lower grade rainforest timber not suitable for sawmilling is salvaged as pulpwood from forest operations, road lines and areas to be flooded. About 100,000 tonnes of rainforest wood is salvaged each year for pulpwood.

Most rainforest timbers are today used in small quantities for effect or decoration, or in wood turning and carving. Their wide variety of hardness, grain, colour and texture has great

▶
This unique dining chair features use of timber from the rainforest scrub species horizontal. Bark has been retained on the upright pieces, while the arms and upper back are made from alternate laminations of horizontal and blackwood. The mid-back and seat are leather. The chair was made by Ross Straker while a wood design student at the School of Art, University of Tasmania. *Photo Uffe Schulze*

Black heart sassafras has been used to construct this buffet. Courtesy Lifestyle Furniture, Hobart. *Photo Uffe Schulze*
▼▶

A myrtle coffee table featuring fiddleback grain. Courtesy Lifestyle Furniture, Hobart. *Photo Uffe Schulze*
▼

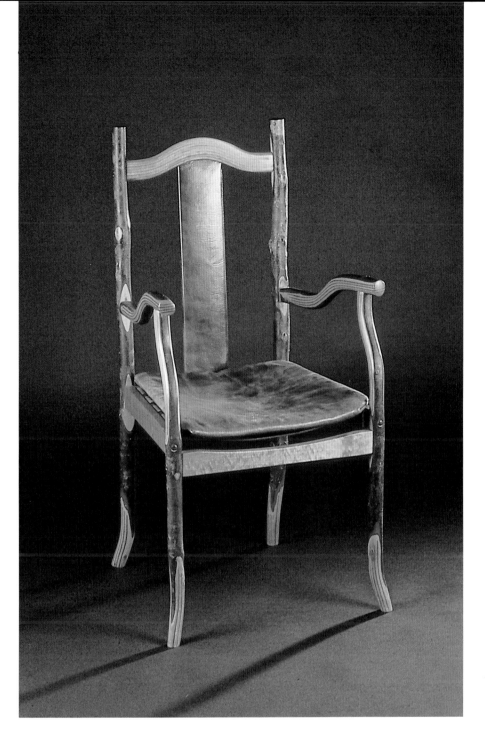

appeal, both to the crafts people and the buying public.

Altogether, about 20 rainforest species are suitable for wood craft. Of the species used solely for craft, three are in steady demand:

- **Horizontal**, which has the unusual characteristic of very tightly-bound bark, and can be turned with the bark on.
- **Dorrel**, which is notable for the attractive colours frequently found in the heartwood.
- **Musk**, whose contorted grain patterns can be cut into spectacularly figured veneers.

Future timber usage: Most of the demand for rainforest species sawlogs can continue to be met for the next two or three decades from the harvesting of mixed forest. After this time future supplies would be available only from rainforest. The feasibility of logging and regenerating rainforest has been researched since the mid-1970s.

Rainforest species generally have very slow growth rates, and with the probable exception of blackwood they cannot economically be grown in plantations. Low-cost techniques to encourage natural regeneration after logging are being developed, concentrating mostly on myrtle and celery top pine.

A series of small logging and regeneration trials in callidendrous rainforest has shown that dense myrtle regeneration can be obtained if seed and shelter trees are retained while removing the sawlogs and most of the pulpwood. Growth of regenerated myrtle is slow compared with that of eucalypts, and about 200 years will be needed for trees of sawlog size in untended stands. Early thinning, however, can improve growth rates to the point where a 100-year rotation age is feasible.

Trial logging of celery top pine in thamnic rainforest has indicated that

the species will regenerate on moderately disturbed sites. But growth rates are very slow, and at least 300 years would be needed to grow trees of sawlog size.

Blackwood timber is being produced in perpetuity through the logging of managed blackwood swamp forest near Smithton. These areas are managed on a rotation of about 70 years.

Huon pine and King Billy pine are not available on a sustainable commercial basis: they are too slow-growing to be considered for economically viable management.

Forest plantations: Plantations of fast

▲
A celery top pine "cone". The small black seeds are partially enclosed within a white aril which is set in a fleshy purple receptacle. Birds eat the receptacles and can disperse the seed over long distances. *Photo Jean Jarman*

◀◀ ▲
Celery top pine regeneration four years after logging in a thamnic rainforest regeneration trial. Seedlings establish well on moderately disturbed peat seedbeds but growth is very slow. *Photo John Hickey*

◀
Myrtle logs are often decayed due to stem-rotting fungi. These logs are not suitable for sawn timber and are taken as pulpwood. The rotted heart of this log is unusual: the cavity has been filled by internal roots which have originated from high up inside the tree trunk. *Photo John Hickey*

▶
Recording diameter growth in a trial plot of thinned myrtle. This stand of dense myrtle regrowth resulted from a small fire in callidendrous rainforest about 40 years ago. Thinning of young myrtle regrowth is expensive but can markedly increase growth rates of retained trees. At this site thinned trees are growing at about 9 mm a year in diameter compared to about 3 mm for adjacent unthinned trees. Thinning in older stands is not feasible, as it can induce myrtle wilt in retained trees as well as excessive windthrow. *Photo John Hickey*

▲

Huon pine, which occurs
naturally only in Tasmania, makes
an important contribution to the
State's craftwood industry.
A Forestry Commission
management policy prescribes a
small annual sawlog cut – 500
cubic metres a year – from
sources such as areas flooded for
hydro-electric purposes, as well as
previously cut over areas forming
about 20 per cent of the total
Huon pine habitat. This supply is
expected to last at least 70 years,

and small amounts of craftwood
will continue to be obtainable for
many decades after sawmilling
ceases. There are about 2500
hectares of vegetation dominated
by Huon pine. About a third of
this is in formal reserves, such as
the Truchanas Nature Reserve,
Franklin and Lower Gordon –
Wild Rivers National Park,
South-West National Park and
the Pieman River State Reserve.
Photo John Pedley

▲

Although a useful timber, King
Billy pine is in small demand, and
there are adequate substitutes for
all of its uses. A Forestry
Commission management policy
allows the salvage of timber from
areas affected by wildfires and
operations such as road
construction and inundation.
Cutting has been restricted to
stands which previously have been
heavily disturbed. Undisturbed
stands will be protected.
Photo Dennis Harding

growing trees such as radiata pine and shining gum have successfully been established on former rainforested land, mainly private property, and the feasibility of blackwood plantations on such land is being examined. Suitable areas for similar future developments would include rainforested land heavily disturbed by past logging or fire and close to existing forest used primarily for wood production.

Tourism

The special characteristics of Tasmanian rainforest – its unique plants and ecology, landscape and rivers – are of great interest to visitors to the State. The tourism potential of rainforest so far remains relatively undeveloped, but there are promising signs for future growth, given careful and imaginative planning.

Many of the best stands of rainforest are far removed from roads, and extended bush walks are needed to view them. However, there are some fine examples fairly close to roads, and a list of these is in *Appendix IV*.

Rainforest has a low tolerance of disturbance, yet most uses of rainforest involve disturbance, some more than others. The impact on the rainforest

▶

Fine stands of rainforest adjoin some roads and tracks in western Tasmania. *Photo Peter Walton*

Cruise boats on the Gordon River provide a popular means of viewing riverine rainforest. *Photo Peter Walton*

▼

environment of tourism, including bush-walking, is minor compared to that of timber harvesting, but it can still cause noticeable local damage. Areas considered to have tourism potential will retain this potential only as long as their natural values are protected.

Leatherwood honey

The honey produced from leatherwood blossom is highly prized for its distinctive flavour. Leatherwood flowers are copious producers of nectar, and most trees blossom over a long period, from December to March. Logging of mixed forest, from which the nectar can also be obtained, makes rainforest increasingly important as a source of nectar. In a good season, leatherwood honey production can be more than 500 tonnes, most of it for export to Europe and the United States.

Horticulture

Public awareness of the unique values of Tasmanian rainforest species has heightened interest in them as garden plants. This has prompted nurseries to collect and stock rainforest plants in increasing numbers and variety, and has given rise to studies of their propagation and care. The discovery that some species grow more quickly under cultivation than in the wild has enhanced their horticultural potential.

Mining

Several of Tasmania's rainforest areas are known to be rich in minerals. The rock type known as Mount Read volcanics, which has provided a good

◀

Leatherwood blossom provides the nectar for Tasmania's leatherwood honey industry. Nectar is obtained commercially from *Eucryphia lucida* (pictured), which is widespread in western Tasmania, and also from a smaller related species, *Eucryphia milliganii*. *Photo Sue Jennings*

deal of Tasmania's past and present mineral wealth, underlies much of the rainforest in western Tasmania. Some of the rarest rainforest communities also occur on Mount Read volcanics.

Hydro-electric developments

Flooding of river valleys in western Tasmania for generation of hydro-electricity usually involves a loss of rainforest. In some cases species or communities with restricted valley habitats can be significantly reduced in area. An example is the habitat of Huon pine, which has been reduced by recent power schemes, although the species cannot be considered endangered. In these cases, while the species habitat is reduced the timber is not wasted: it is salvaged and stockpiled to be released to the market over a period of years.

Agriculture

Most rainforest clearing for agriculture occurred in north-western Tasmania, especially on fertile basalt soils. Most of this land was cleared before the 1930s, and is now used for dairying and vegetable production. Since then, small parcels of rainforested Crown land have been sold to private owners for agricultural use.

▲
Native laurel is grown from cuttings for horticultural purposes. It has delicate white flowers and large, glossy leaves, and is easily established in gardens, growing as a shrub or small tree. Other rainforest species grown as garden plants include leatherwood, King Billy pine, climbing heath and *Trochocarpa gunnii*. Courtesy Westlands Nursery, Hobart.
Photo John Hickey

▶
Aerial roots are sometimes found on whitey wood (*Acradenia frankliniae*), a species found in gallery and floodbank rainforest on some western and south-western rivers. *Photo Jean Jarman*

◀
A native laurel sapling as it appears in its rainforest habitat.
Photo Rob Blakers

8

RAINFOREST·MANAGEMENT

◀

Cephissus Creek, Pine Valley, in
the Cradle Mountain-Lake St
Clair National Park.
Photo Dennis Harding

8 RAINFOREST·MANAGEMENT

Slender tree fern, *Cyathea cunninghamii*, in a relic rainforest patch in eastern Tasmania. Only a few widely spread individuals of this species have been found in Tasmania, in mixed forest and rainforested gullies, although it also occurs in Victoria. Unlike the common manfern, it is believed to be easily killed by fire.
Photo Michael Garrett

Old Mans Beard, *Usnea* sp., hangs in festoons from the limbs of old myrtle trees. It is one of about 200 macrolichen species found in rainforest.
Photo Gintaras Kantvilas

▼▶

Papillaria flavo-limbata is one of many moss species found in rainforest. Little is known of their reservation status.
Photo Jean Jarman

▼

Management of rainforest, like that of any other forest resource, requires a balance between uses of various kinds and total preservation so that the resource is conserved. Conservation, as defined by the National Conservation Strategy for Australia, is "the management of human use of the biosphere so that it may yield the greatest sustainable benefit to present generations while maintaining its potential to meet the needs and aspirations of future generations".

Productive uses of rainforest have been discussed in the previous chapter, but there are several non-commercial reasons why Tasmanian rainforest needs to be conserved:

- to protect the plants and animals which make up the forest;

- to provide examples of relatively undisturbed ecosystems for comparison with modified ones;
- to protect scientific evidence, discovered and potential; and
- to meet educational, recreational and inspirational desires.

The future

Views vary widely as to how rainforest should be managed. Governments and land managers are faced with the task of protecting the rainforest so that it can thrive in all its variety, while enabling legitimate and reasonable community needs to be met. Considered, sensitive and far sighted management is the challenge on which depends the survival of this irreplaceable resource.

▶

Photo Peter Walton

The Tasmanian Government set up the Working Group for Rainforest Conservation to give advice on rainforest conservation needs. The Working Group, consisting of people from the Forestry Commission and the Department of Lands, Parks and Wildlife, was asked to study rainforest communities of Tasmania and recommend appropriate conservation measures.

The Working Group divided Tasmania into 11 Nature Conservation Regions. Rainforest within each region is being classified according to its reservation status, within geological and altitudinal zones. Where current provision for conservation is inadequate, further representative areas will be recommended for reservation.

The Group has also collated information on the locations of rainforest communities. In some cases reserves will be recommended for rare communities, such as those containing King Billy pine, diselma and deciduous beech. The status of individual species is also being examined. At least nine seed plants and eight fern species are thought to be poorly reserved, and little is known about the conservation status of lower plants such as mosses and lichens.

FURTHER·READING

*The following books and articles provide an entry into the quite extensive literature about Tasmanian rainforest. They are grouped according to their area of interest. Some are out of print but are available from libraries.

GENERAL	ANON (1983)	**Tasmanian Rainforests – Recent Research Results,** F.E.R.F, Hobart
	BEADLE, N.C.W. (1981).	**The Vegetation of Australia,** Cambridge University Press, Cambridge, U.K.
	BLAKERS, R. and ROBERTSON, P. (eds) (1983).	**Tasmania's Rainforests: What Future?** A.C.F., Hobart
	BROWN, M.J., KIRKPATRICK, J.B. and MOSCAL, A. (1983).	**An Atlas of Tasmania's Endemic Flora.** Tasmanian Conservation Trust Inc., Hobart
	CASSON, P.B. (1952).	The forests of Western Tasmania. **Australian Forestry** 16: 71-86
	HOWARD, T.M. (1981).	Southern closed-forests. In R.J. Groves (ed), **Australian Vegetation**, Cambridge University Press, Cambridge : 102-120
	JACKSON, W.D. (1965).	Vegetation. In J.L. Davies (ed), **Atlas of Tasmania,** Department of Lands and Surveys, Hobart: 30-35
	JARMAN, S.J. and BROWN, M.J. (1983).	A definition of cool temperate rainforest in Tasmania. **Search** 14: 81-87
	JARMAN, S.J., BROWN, M.J. and KANTVILAS, G. (1984).	**Rainforest in Tasmania**, National Parks and Wildlife Service, Tasmania
	KIRKPATRICK, J.B. (1977).	Native vegetation of the West Coast region of Tasmania. In M.R. Banks and J.B. Kirkpatrick (eds), **Landscape and Man**, Proceedings of a symposium of the Royal Society of Tasmania: 55-80
	KIRKPATRICK, J.B. and DICKINSON, K.J.M. (1984).	**Vegetation Map of Tasmania 1:500,000,** Forestry Commission, Hobart.
	WEBB. L.J., TRACEY, J.G. and WILLIAMS, W.T. (1984).	A floristic framework of Australian rainforests. **Australian Journal of Ecology** 9: 167-198
OTHER CATEGORIES Animals	RICHARDSON, A.M.M., ROUNSEVELL, D.E. and HOCKING, G.J. (1984).	Status of Tasmanian rainforest fauna. In Werren, G.L. and Kershaw, A.P. (eds), **Australian National Rainforest Study, Report to the World Wildlife Fund (Australia), Vol. I : Proceedings of a workshop on the past, present and future of Australian rainforests** (Griffith University, December 1983), Geography Department, Monash University, Melbourne, for the Australian Conservation Foundation: 345-357

Dendrochronology

FRANCEY, R.J. and others (1984).

Isotopes in tree rings. **Division of Atmospheric Research Technical Paper 4**, C.S.I.R.O., Australia

LA MARCHE, V.C. Jr. and PITTOCK, A.B. (1981).

Preliminary temperature reconstructions for Tasmania. In M.K. Hughes, P.M. Kelly, J.R. Pilcher and V.C. La Marche Jr. (eds), **Climate from Tree Rings**, Cambridge University Press: 177-185

Ecology

BUSBY, J.R. (1986).

A biogeoclimatic analysis of *Nothofagus cunninghamii* (Hook.) Oerst. in south-eastern Australia. **Australian Journal of Ecology** 2: 1-7

CULLEN, P.J. (1987).

Regeneration patterns in populations of *Athrotaxis selaginoides* D. Don. from Tasmania. **Journal of Biogeography** 14: 39-51

ELLIS, R.C. (1985).

The relationships among eucalypt forest, grasslands and rainforest in a highland area in north-eastern Tasmania. **Australian Journal of Ecology** 10: 197-314

JACKSON, W.D. (1968).

Fire, air, water and earth – an elemental ecology of Tasmania. **Proceedings of the Ecological Society of Australia** 3: 9-16

KIRKPATRICK, J.B. (1984).

Altitudinal and successional variation in the vegetation of the northern part of the West Coast Range, Tasmania. **Australian Journal of Ecology** 9: 81-91

READ, J. (1985).

Photosynthetic and growth responses to different light regimes of the major canopy species of Tasmanian cool temperate rainforest. **Australian Journal of Ecology** 10: 327-334

READ, J. and HILL, R.S. (1985).

Dynamics of *Nothofagus*-dominated rainforest on mainland Australia and lowland Tasmania. **Vegetatio** 63: 67-78

Fire

BROWN, M.J. and PODGER, F.D. (1982).

Floristics and fire regimes of a vegetation sequence from sedgeland heath to rainforest at Bathurst Harbour, Tasmania. **Australian Journal of Botany** 30: 659-76

HILL, R.S. and READ, J. (1984).

Post-fire regeneration of rainforest and mixed forest in Western Tasmania. **Australian Journal of Botany** 32: 481-493

MOUNT, A.B. (1979).

Natural regeneration processes in Tasmanian forests. **Search** 10: 180-186

Forest Management

CALAIS, S.S. and KIRKPATRICK, J.B. (1983).

Tree species regeneration after logging in temperate rainforest, Tasmania. **Papers and Proceedings of the Royal Society of Tasmania** 117: 77-83

FORESTRY COMMISSION, TASMANIA (1982).

Draft Blackwood Working Plan.

FORESTRY COMMISSION, TASMANIA (1987).

Policy for management of Huon pine

FORESTRY COMMISSION, TASMANIA (1987).

Policy for management of King Billy pine

	DUNCAN, F. (1986).	**Tasmania's vegetation and its response to forest operations. Working Paper No. 6: background information additional to the Environmental Impact Statement on Tasmanian Woodchip Exports Beyond 1988,** Forestry Commission, Hobart
	GIBSON, N. (1986).	**Conservation and management of Huon pine in Tasmania.** Wildlife Division Technical Report 86/3, National Parks and Wildlife Service, Tasmania
	HICKEY, J.E. (1984).	Management and silviculture of Tasmania's rainforest. In Werren, G.L. and Kershaw, A.P. (eds), **Australian National Rainforest Study, Report to the World Wildlife Fund (Australia), Vol. I : Proceedings of a workshop on the past, present and future of Australian rainforests** (Griffith University, December 1983), Geography Department, Monash University, Melbourne, for the Australian Conservation Foundation : 614-616
Palaeobotany	HILL, R.S. and MACPHAIL, M.K. (1985).	A fossil flora from rafted Plio-pleistocene mudstones at Regatta Point, Tasmania. **Australian Journal of Botany** 33: 497-517
	MACPHAIL, M.K. (1979).	Vegetation and climates in southern Tasmania since the last glaciation. **Quaternary Research** 11: 306-341
	MACPHAIL, M.K. and HILL, R.S. (1983).	Cool temperate rainforest in Tasmania: a reply. **Search** 14: 186-187
	PLAYFORD, G., and DETTMANN, M.E. (1979).	Pollen of *Dacrydium franklinii* Hook. f. and comparable early Tertiary microfossils. **Pollen et spores** 20: 513-534
Pests and Diseases	ELLIOTT, H.J., KILE, G.A., CANDY, S.G. and RATKOWSKY D.A. (1986).	Incidence and spatial pattern of *Nothofagus cunninghamii* (Hook.) Oerst. attacked by *Platypus subgranosus* Schell in Tasmania's cool temperate rainforest. **Australian Journal of Ecology** 12(2): 125-138
	KILE, G.A. and WALKER, J. (1987).	*Chalara australis* sp. nov. (Hyphomycetes), a vascular pathogen of *Nothofagus cunninghamii* (Fagaceae) in Australia and its relationship to other *Chalara* spp. **Australian Journal of Botany** 35: 1-32
Plants	JARMAN, S.J., KANTVILAS, G. and BROWN, M.J. (1986).	The ecology of pteridophytes in Tasmanian cool temperate rainforest. **The Fern Gazette** 13(2) : 77-86
	KANTVILAS, G., JAMES, P.W. and JARMAN, S.J. (1985).	Macrolichens in Tasmanian rainforests. **Lichenologist** 17(1): 67-83

GLOSSARY OF COMMON NAMES

The following list provides scientific names for all species referred to in the text. It is not a complete list of plants and animals occurring in rainforest, and includes some non-rainforest species.

	COMMON NAME	SCIENTIFIC NAME
PLANTS	blackwood	*Acacia melanoxylon*
	blanket leaf, blanket bush	*Bedfordia salicina*
	celery top pine	*Phyllocladus aspleniifolius*
	climbing heath	*Prionotes cerinthoides*
	deciduous beech	*Nothofagus gunnii*
	diselma (Cheshunt pine)	*Diselma archeri*
	dorrel	*Notelaea ligustrina*
	fagus	*Nothofagus gunnii*
	hard water fern	*Blechnum wattsii*
	horizontal	*Anodopetalum biglandulosum*
	Huon pine	*Lagarostrobos franklinii*
	King Billy pine	*Athrotaxis selaginoides*
	lancewood	*Phebalium squameum*
	leatherwood	*Eucryphia lucida*
	leatherwood (dwarf)	*Eucryphia milliganii*
	manfern	*Dicksonia antarctica*
	mother shield fern	*Polystichum proliferum*
	mountain pepper	*Tasmannia lanceolata*
	musk	*Olearia argophylla*
	myrtle	*Nothofagus cunninghamii*
	native laurel	*Anopterus glandulosus*
	native olive	*Notelaea ligustrina*
	native pear	*Pomaderris apetala*
	native plum	*Cenarrhenes nitida*
	pandani	*Richea pandanifolia*
	paperbark	*Melaleuca spp.*
	pencil pine	*Athrotaxis cupressoides*
	radiata pine	*Pinus radiata*
	sassafras	*Atherosperma moschatum*
	scoparia	*Richea scoparia*
	soft treefern	*Dicksonia antarctica*
	shining gum	*Eucalyptus nitens*
	stringy bark	*Eucalyptus obliqua*
	teatree	*Leptospermum spp.*
	waratah	*Telopea truncata*
	white waratah	*Agastachys odorata*

COMMON NAME	SCIENTIFIC NAME
whitey wood	*Acradenia frankliniae*
woolly teatree	*Leptospermum lanigerum*

ANIMALS

COMMON NAME	SCIENTIFIC NAME
black currawong	*Strepera fuliginosa*
blotched blue-tongued lizard	*Tiliqua nigrolutea*
brown skink	*Leiolopisma metallica*
brown tree frog	*Litoria ewingii*
brush bronzewing	*Phaps elegans*
cat (domestic)	*Felis cattus*
chocolate bat	*Chalinolobus morio*
common froglet	*Ranidella signifera*
collared sparrowhawk	*Accipiter cirrhocephalus*
crescent honeyeater	*Phylidonyris pyrrhoptera*
dusky antechinus	*Antechinus swainsonii*
eastern spinebill	*Acanthorhynchus tenuirostris*
echidna	*Tachyglossus aculeatus*
forest raven	*Corvus tasmanicus*
golden whistler	*Pachycephala pectoralis*
green rosella	*Platycercus caledonicus*
grey fantail	*Rhipidura fuliginosa*
grey goshawk	*Accipiter novaehollandiae*
grey shrike thrush	*Colluricincla harmonica*
lesser long-eared bat	*Nyctophilus geoffroyi*
little forest bat	*Eptesicus saggitula*
long-tailed mouse	*Pseudomys higginsii*
long-tailed rat	*Pseudomys higginsii*
marsupial mouse	*Antechinus swainsonii*
masked owl	*Tyto novaehollandiae*
mountain pinhole borer	*Platypus subgranosus*
mouse (European)	*Mus musculus*
oak skink	*Tiliqua casuarinae*
ocellated skink	*Leiolopisma ocellatum*
olive whistler	*Pachycephala olivacea*
pademelon	*Thylogale billardierii*
pink robin	*Petroica rodinogaster*
ringtail possum	*Pseudocheirus peregrinus*
rufous wallaby	*Thylogale billardierii*
scrubtit	*Sericornis magnus*
shining bronze cuckoo	*Chrysococcyx lucidus*
silvereye	*Zosterops latesalis*
southern boobook	*Ninox novaeseelandiae*
spotted-tail quoll	*Dasyurus maculatus*
swamp rat	*Rattus lutreolus*
Tasmanian devil	*Sarcophilus harrisii*
Tasmanian froglet	*Ranidella tasmaniensis*

Tasmanian thornbill	*Acanthiza ewingii*
Tasmanian tree frog	*Litoria burrowsi*
tiger cat	*Dasyurus maculatus*
tiger snake	*Notechis ater*
white-breasted sea eagle	*Haliaeetus leucogaster*
white-browed scrub wren	*Sericornis frontalis*
white-lipped whip snake	*Drysdalia coronoides*
Whites thrush	*Zoothera dauma*
yellow-tailed black cockatoo	*Calyptorhynchus funereus*
yellow-throated honeyeater	*Lichenostomus flavicollis*

CHECKLIST OF THE HIGHER PLANTS IN TASMANIAN RAINFOREST*

*After Jarman, Brown and Kantvilas, 1984

The following species have been commonly recorded in Tasmanian cool temperate rainforest. For convenience they are grouped within their **primary division** (angiosperms, gymnosperms or pteridophytes) and listed alphabetically according to their **genus** (the first part of their scientific name) and their **species** (the second part), with common names added where they exist.

Angiosperms, the most highly evolved group, are plants whose seeds are enclosed in an ovary – the flowering plants. The angiosperms of the rainforest include some of the best-known trees such as myrtle, sassafras and leatherwood, as well as smaller plants such as the heaths, berries, and grasses. In the list below, angiosperms are divided into **monocotyledons** (plants with only one cotyledon, or seed leaf, including grasses, sedges and orchids) and **dicotyledons** (plants with two cotyledons, including woody plants).

Gymnosperms, or conifers, are plants with exposed seeds. In Tasmanian rainforest they are basically the pine trees, including celery-top, pencil, Huon and King Billy.

The third major group consists of the **pteridophytes**, which comprise ferns, with other related primitive plants. The prominent pteridophytes of the rainforest include manferns, water ferns, mother shield ferns and filmy ferns.

Each of these primary divisions contains a number of smaller groups called families (not shown), which contain related genera and species. Angiosperms are represented by 32 families in Tasmanian rainforest, gymnosperms by three families, and pteridophytes by 16.

Asterisks (*) indicate species that are restricted to rainforest, mixed forest and alpine environments. Rainforest species without asterisks also occur commonly in other moist vegetation types such as wet sclerophyll forest and blackwood swamp forest.

Plus signs (+) indicate species found naturally only in Tasmania.

	SCIENTIFIC/COMMON NAMES	NOTES
ANGIOSPERMAE **Monocotyledons**	***Acianthus viridis** *(Tasmanian beech orchid)*	Small orchid, sporadic but widely distributed
	Carex appressa	Wiry tufted sedge up to 1 m high in gallery rainforest or disturbed situations; mostly in callidendrous and thamnic rainforest
	Chiloglottis cornuta *(green bird orchid)*	Small orchid in callidendrous rainforest
	Dianella tasmanica *(blueberry)*	Lily, mainly in mixed forest but sometimes scattered in thamnic rainforest

	SCIENTIFIC/COMMON NAMES	NOTES
	Drymophila cyanocarpa *(turquoise berry)*	Small lily, scattered in thamnic, callidendrous and sometimes implicate rainforest
	Gahnia grandis *(cutting grass)*	Large rosette sedge, widespread in rainforest but most vigorous in implicate rainforest; it becomes depauperate under dense forest canopies
	Lepidosperma sp. *(sword sedge)*	Large rosette sedge; status unclear in rainforest
	Libertia pulchella *(liberty grass)*	Small, soft-leaved iris in callidendrous and thamnic rainforest; common near creeks, in moist situations and in some high altitude situations
	Pterostylis sp. *(greenhood)*	Small orchid, occasional in rainforest
	Scirpus sp.	Small, fine leafed sedge, present in gallery rainforest and in rainforest bogs.
	Uncinia riparia *(river hook sedge)*	Grass-like sedge in gallery rainforest
	U. tenella *(delicate hook sedge)*	Small grass-like sedge, widespread in rainforest
Dicotyledons	**Acacia dealbata** *(silver wattle)*	Tree, gallery rainforest and callidendrous rainforest in north-eastern Tasmania
	A. melanoxylon *(blackwood)*	Tree, mostly in callidendrous and thamnic rainforest. May be common in floodbank or gallery communities. It is sporadic away from rivers, where disturbances open the canopy.
	A. mucronata *(native willow)*	Shrub or small tree, sometimes common in implicate rainforest
	A. verticillata *(prickly mimosa)*	Shrub or small tree, mostly in gallery rainforest
	***+Acradenia frankliniae** *(whitey wood)*	Small tree in floodbank and gallery rainforest. Restricted to few large rivers and their tributaries in the west and south-west
	+Agastachys odorata *(white waratah)*	Tall shrub, common in implicate rainforest
	***+Anodopetalum biglandulosum** *(horizontal)*	Tall shrub or small tree, widespread and common in thamnic and implicate rainforest
	***+Anopterus glandulosus** *(native laurel)*	Medium to tall shrub, sometimes a small slender tree; mainly in thamnic and implicate rainforest
	***+Archeria eriocarpa**	Medium to tall shrub, mostly in thamnic rainforest in communities near streams or at higher altitudes, possibly where frequent mists occur
	***+A. hirtella**	Medium to tall shrub, confined to thamnic and implicate rainforest
	***+A. serpyllifolia**	Medium shrub, in high altitude implicate rainforest
	+Aristotelia peduncularis *(heart berry)*	Low to tall spindly shrub, widespread but sporadic throughout rainforest communities

SCIENTIFIC/COMMON NAMES	NOTES
*Atherosperma moschatum (sassafras)	Tree, widespread and common in callidendrous and thamnic rainforest; also present in implicate rainforest, but usually represented by small or depauperate individuals
Australina pusilla	Small, soft, straggling herb, restricted to callidendrous rainforest
Callitriche brachycarpa	Small prostrate herb colonising shaded bogs in rainforest
*+Cenarrhenes nitida (native plum)	Medium to tall shrub, sometimes a small tree; common in thamnic and implicate rainforest
Clematis aristata (clematis)	Woody climber, mostly in gallery rainforest or disturbed edges
Coprosma nitida	Medium to tall shrub, mostly in implicate and open montane rainforest
C. quadrifida (native currant)	Small to tall shrub, mostly in callidendrous rainforest and sometimes in thamnic floodbank rainforest
Correa lawrenciana	Medium to tall shrub
+Cyathodes glauca (cheeseberry)	Medium shrub, scattered in rainforest at medium to high altitudes; status in rainforest unclear
C. juniperina	Medium to tall shrub, often in implicate rainforest but also sporadic in thamnic rainforest
*+Epacris mucronulata	Medium shrub, restricted to gallery rainforest; occurs only on some of the larger rivers and creeks
*+Eucryphia lucida (leatherwood)	Tree, most characteristic of thamnic rainforest but also present in implicate rainforest and in some callidendrous rainforest
*+E. milliganii	Low tree, present in thamnic and implicate rainforest
Galium australe	Soft straggling herb, occasional in high altitude rainforest
+Gaultheria hispida (snow berry)	Small shrub, mostly associated with rainforest edges, local disturbances or gallery rainforest
Hydrocotyle javanica	Small creeping herb, found mostly in moist situations, particularly disturbed sites in callidendrous rainforest; sometimes common in gallery rainforest
H. pterocarpa	Small creeping herb, found mostly in moist situations in thamnic and implicate rainforest; sometimes common in gallery rainforest
Lagenophora stipitata	Small rosette herb, often in gallery rainforest or high altitude callidendrous rainforest
Leptospermum lanigerum (woolly teatree)	Tree, present in implicate rainforest or high altitude callidendrous rainforest, often in poorly drained situations
L. nitidum	Tree, restricted to implicate rainforest
*+L. riparium	Medium to tall shrub, restricted to gallery rainforest on a few of the larger rivers
L. scoparium (manuka)	Tree, confined to implicate rainforest
Melaleuca squarrosa (paper bark)	Tree, confined to implicate rainforest

SCIENTIFIC/COMMON NAMES	NOTES
+**Monotoca glauca**	Tall shrub or small tree, scattered, mostly in thamnic rainforest
+**M. submutica**	Tall shrub, confined to implicate rainforest
Notelaea ligustrina (*dorrel, native olive*)	Tall shrub to small tree, mostly scattered in thamnic rainforest and gallery rainforest
*__Nothofagus cunninghamii__ (*myrtle*)	Tree, widespread
*+**N. gunnii** (*deciduous beech*)	Medium shrub to tall tree, mostly in implicate and open montane rainforest but also (rarely) in thamnic rainforest
Olearia argophylla (*musk*)	Medium to tall shrub, restricted to callidendrous rainforest
+**O. persoonioides**	Medium shrub in implicate rainforest
*+**O. pinifolia**	Medium shrub restricted to open montane rainforest
+**Orites diversifolia**	Medium to tall shrub, found mostly in thamnic rainforest but sometimes in implicate rainforest
Oxalis lactea	Small clover-like herb present in gallery rainforest and in high altitude callidendrous and thamnic rainforest
*+**Pimelea cinerea**	Medium to low slender shrub, sometimes sporadic in gallery rainforest and callidendrous rainforest
P. drupacea	Medium to low slender shrub, widespread in callidendrous rainforest
Pittosporum bicolor (*cheesewood, tallow wood*)	Tall shrub to small tree, widespread but sporadic in callidendrous and thamnic rainforest but also present sometimes in other groups
*+**Prionotes cerinthoides** (*climbing heath*)	Small, often epiphytic shrub, abundant in implicate rainforest and in some thamnic communities
*+**Pseudopanax gunnii** (*native ivy bush*)	Small shrub, sporadic in implicate rainforest
*+**Richea milliganii**	Medium shrub, present in some implicate communities
*+**R. pandanifolia** (*pandani*)	Medium to tall rosette shrub or small tree; common in implicate and thamnic and in some open montane rainforest
*+**R. scoparia** (*scoparia*)	Medium to tall shrub, present in high altitude implicate and open montane rainforest
Tasmannia lanceolata (*mountain pepper*)	Medium to tall shrub or small tree; widespread in rainforest but most prominent in high altitude callidendrous rainforest
+**Telopea truncata** (*waratah*)	Medium to tall shrub or small tree; widespread in rainforest but most prominent in high altitude callidendrous communities
*+**Tetracarpaea tasmanica**	Small shrub in implicate rainforest
*+**Trochocarpa cunninghamii**	Low to medium shrub, sometimes scrambling; common in thamnic and implicate rainforest but also in some high altitude callidendrous rainforest
+**T. disticha**	Low to medium shrub, similar to T. cunninghamii but more robust; present in thamnic and implicate rainforest in the far south

	SCIENTIFIC/COMMON NAMES	NOTES
	*+T. gunnii	Medium to tall shrub, mostly in thamnic or implicate rainforest
	Urtica incisa *(stinging nettle)*	Stinging herb, often associated with disturbed sites
	Viola hederacea *(ivy-leaf violet)*	Small herb, sometimes common in gallery rainforest
GYMNOSPERMAE	***+Athrotaxis cupressoides** *(pencil pine)*	Small tree, mostly in open montane rainforest and high altitude gallery rainforest
	*+A. laxifolia	Small tree, presumed to be a hybrid between *A. cupressoides* and *A. selaginoides*
	*+A. selaginoides *(King Billy pine)*	Small to tall tree, in thamnic and implicate rainforest
	*+Diselma archeri *(diselma or Cheshunt pine)*	Medium to tall shrub, sometimes a small tree; mostly in implicate and open montane rainforests
	*+Lagarostrobos franklinii *(Huon pine)*	Tree, present in mid to low altitude thamnic and implicate rainforest
	*+Microstrobos niphophilus	Low to medium shrub, restricted to open montane rainforest
	*+Phyllocladus aspleniifolius *(celery top pine)*	Tree, widespread in rainforest but most typical of thamnic and implicate rainforest
PTERIDOPHYTA	***+Apteropteris applanata** *(skeleton filmy fern)*	Small fern, mainly epiphytic on *Athrotaxis* trunks but sometimes also on rock faces
	Asplenium bulbiferum *(mother spleenwort)*	Uncommon in rainforest; mainly on rockfaces
	A. flabellifolium *(necklace fern)*	Uncommon in rainforest; occasionally found on well-lit rockfaces or in rock crevices
	A. flaccidum *(weeping spleenwort)*	Epiphyte, sporadic in callidendrous and thamnic rainforest
	A. trichomanes *(common spleenwort)*	Small ground fern restricted to limestone rocks
	Blechnum chambersii *(lance water fern)*	Ground fern, occasional in very shaded situations along creek margins and on rockfaces
	B. fluviatile *(ray water fern)*	Ground fern along creek margins
	B. minus *(soft water fern)*	Ground fern along the margins of some of the larger creeks and rivers
	B. nudum *(fishbone water fern)*	Common ground fern in gallery rainforest
	B. penna-marina *(alpine water fern)*	Scattered in callidendrous rainforest at higher altitudes

SCIENTIFIC/COMMON NAMES	NOTES
B. vulcanicum (*wedge water fern*)	Ground fern, mostly in gallery rainforest along the larger creeks and rivers but sometimes present also on rockfaces
B. wattsii (*hard water fern*)	Common ground fern, particularly in thamnic and implicate rainforest but also present in some callidendrous rainforest
***Ctenopteris heterophylla** (*gypsy fern*)	Epiphytic fern, found in thamnic and callidendrous rainforest
Cyathea australis (*rough tree fern*)	Tree fern, mainly in relic patches of rainforest in eastern Tasmania
Dicksonia antarctica (*manfern*)	Tree fern, common in callidendrous rainforest but also in thamnic rainforest mostly near creeks or in wet areas
***Diplazium australe** (*austral lady fern*)	Ground fern, mostly recorded from rainforests of the north-west
Grammitis billardieri (*finger fern*)	Common epiphytic fern, widespread in all groups except open montane rainforest
G. magellanica	Occasional epiphyte in callidendrous and thamnic rainforest.
Histiopteris incisa (*bat's wing fern*)	Ground fern, occasional under closed canopies but common in disturbed situations; mostly restricted to callidendrous rainforest; sometimes common in gallery rainforest
***Hymenophyllum australe** (*austral filmy fern*)	Small fern, usually in moist situations; sometimes epiphytic on buttresses but mostly a ground species; widespread in callidendrous and thamnic rainforest and also found in implicate rainforest
***H. cupressiforme** (*common filmy fern*)	Small epiphytic species, in callidendrous and thamnic rainforest
***H. flabellatum** (*shiny filmy fern*)	Largest of the Tasmanian filmy ferns; mostly epiphytic on tree fern trunks but also on logs and rockfaces; most common in callidendrous rainforest but also sometimes in thamnic rainforest
***H. marginatum** (*bordered filmy fern*)	Very small filmy fern resembling a liverwort; usually epiphytic and found most commonly in implicate or gallery rainforest
***H. peltatum** (*alpine filmy fern*)	Small fern, either epiphytic or ground-dwelling; present in all rainforest groups and across a wide range of altitudes, though most abundant at high elevations
***H. rarum** (*narrow filmy fern*)	Small fern, very common in all rainforest groups except open montane
Hypolepis rugosula (*ruddy ground fern*)	Ground fern, often growing with *Histiopteris*
Lastreopsis hispida (*bristly shield fern*)	Rare, restricted in Tasmania to the North-West
Lindsaea trichomanoides (*oval wedge fern*)	Rare. In Tasmania occurs in thamnic rainforest on Gordon River; also recorded in New River area
Lycopodium fastigiatum (*slender club moss*)	Ground species present in high altitude callidendrous rainforest

SCIENTIFIC/COMMON NAMES	NOTES
L. myrtifolium *(long club moss)*	Epiphytic or terrestrial club moss, occasional in rainforest
Microsorium diversifolium *(kangaroo fern)*	Creeping fern, mainly epiphytic; often on dead standing trees or rotted stumps in callidendrous and thamnic rainforest; rarely in implicate rainforest
*Polyphlebium venosum *(veined bristle fern)*	Small epiphytic fern, restricted to tree fern trunks
Polystichum proliferum *(mother shield fern)*	Common ground fern in callidendrous rainforest
*Pteris comans *(netted brake)*	Uncommon ground fern in rainforest; mostly recorded in north-west
*Rumohra adiantiformis *(leathery shield fern)*	Usually epiphytic in callidendrous and thamnic rainforest
Sticherus lobatus *(spreading fan fern)*	Uncommon in rainforest; mainly in north-west Tasmania but also recorded from north-east
S. tener *(silky fan fern)*	Ground fern, often in disturbed situations and in gallery rainforest
*Tmesipteris billardieri *(long fork fern)*	Mostly an epiphyte on tree fern trunks but sometimes also in peaty soil around tree buttresses
*T. elongata	Epiphytic on tree fern trunks; recorded sporadically in north-west
Todea barbara *(king fern)*	Localised in rainforest

RAINFOREST COMMUNITIES IN TASMANIA*

*After Jarman, Brown and Kantvilas, 1984

Communities frequently intermix, resulting in continuous variation within the rainforest. The following list is best considered as a guide to the most clearly recognisable communities.

CALLIDENDROUS RAINFOREST	**C1**	**Manfern and mother shield fern understoreys:**
	C1a	**Callidendrous fern rainforest:** myrtle and sassafras over manfern
	C1b	**Callidendrous myrtle-musk rainforest:** myrtle and sassafras over musk, manfern and mother shield fern
	C1c	**Callidendrous sassafras-musk rainforest:** sassafras over musk, manfern and mother shield fern
	C2	**Clear understoreys, sometimes with scattered shrubs:**
	C2a	**High altitude callidendrous rainforest:** myrtle and sometimes woolly teatree over clear understoreys or waratah and/or mountain pepper
	C3	**Diselma understoreys:** **Callidendrous pencil pine rainforest:** pencil pine and myrtle over diselma

THAMNIC RAINFOREST	**T1**	**Horizontal understoreys:**
	T1a	**Thamnic horizontal rainforest:** myrtle and leatherwood and sometimes celery top pine over horizontal
	T1b	**Thamnic horizontal rainforest with pandani:** myrtle and leatherwood and sometimes celery top pine over horizontal and pandani
	T1c	**Thamnic horizontal rainforest with King Billy pine:** King Billy pine over horizontal and sometimes pandani
	T1d	**Thamnic horizontal rainforest with Huon pine:** Huon pine and myrtle over horizontal
	T2	**Whitey wood understoreys:**
	T2a	**Thamnic whitey wood rainforest with leatherwood:** myrtle and leatherwood over whitey wood
	T2b	**Thamnic whitey wood rainforest with Huon pine:** Huon pine and myrtle over whitey wood
	T3	**Native laurel and/or native plum understoreys:**
	T3a	**Thamnic laurel rainforest:** myrtle and leatherwood and sometimes celery top pine over native laurel and/or native plum
	T3b	**Thamnic laurel rainforest with Huon pine:** Huon pine and sometimes myrtle over native laurel
	T4	*Archeria* **understoreys:**
	T4a	**Thamnic *Archeria* rainforest:** myrtle and leatherwood over *Archeria eriocarpa*
	T4b	**Thamnic *Archeria* rainforest with Huon pine:** Huon pine and sometimes myrtle over *Archeria eriocarpa*
	T4c	**Thamnic *Archeria* rainforest with King Billy pine:** King Billy pine and sometimes myrtle and *Eucryphia milliganii* over *Archeria eriocarpa* and pandani
	T5	*Trochocarpa gunnii* **understoreys:**
	T5a	**Thamnic *Trochocarpa gunnii* rainforest:** myrtle over *Trochocarpa gunnii*
	T5b	**Thamnic *Trochocarpa gunnii* and pandani rainforest:** King Billy pine and/or myrtle over *Trochocarpa gunnii* and pandani

	T5c	**Thamnic deciduous beech and *Trochocarpa gunnii* rainforest:** King Billy pine and deciduous beech over *Trochocarpa gunnii* and sometimes pandani
	T6	***Trochocarpa cunninghamii* understoreys:**
	T6a	**Thamnic *Trochocarpa cunninghamii* rainforest:** myrtle and celery top pine over *Trochocarpa cunninghamii*
	T6b	**Thamnic *Trochocarpa cunninghamii* rainforest with King Billy pine:** King Billy pine over *Trochocarpa cunninghamii*
IMPLICATE RAINFOREST	**I1**	**White waratah tangled understoreys:**
	I1a	**Implicate white waratah rainforest with celery top pine:** celery top pine and myrtle and sometimes teatree and paperbark species over mixed white waratah tangle
	I1b	**Implicate white waratah rainforest with Huon pine:** Huon pine and myrtle and sometimes teatree and paperbark species over mixed white waratah tangle
	I1c	**Implicate white waratah rainforest with King Billy pine and pandani:** King Billy pine over mixed white waratah tangle with pandani
	I1d	**Implicate white waratah rainforest with King Billy pine and scoparia:** King Billy pine over mixed white waratah tangle with scoparia
	I2	**Deciduous beech understoreys:**
	I2a	**Implicate deciduous beech rainforest:** King Billy pine and diselma over mixed deciduous beech tangle
	I3	**Myrtle and scoparia scrub understoreys:**
	I3a	**Implicate myrtle-scoparia rainforest with King Billy pine:** King Billy pine over myrtle and scoparia scrub
	I4	***Trochocarpa* and climbing heath understoreys:**
	I4a	**Implicate *Trochocarpa* and climbing heath rainforest:** celery top pine and myrtle over *Trochocarpa* species and climbing heath
	I5	**Native laurel and horizontal understoreys:**
	I5a	**Implicate woolly teatree rainforest:** woolly teatree, celery top pine and myrtle over mixed native laurel and horizontal tangle
OPEN MONTANE RAINFOREST	**OM1**	**Montane pencil pine forest with deciduous beech:** pencil pine over deciduous beech and pandani
	OM2	**Montane pencil pine forest over coniferous heath:** pencil pine over coniferous heath
	OM3	**Montane pencil pine forest over heath:** pencil pine over heath with species of the families *Proteaceae* and *Myrtaceae*
	OM4	**Montane pencil pine forest over grassland:** pencil pine over grassland
GALLERY RAINFOREST	**G1**	**Gallery forest with *Leptospermum riparium* scrub**
INTERMEDIATE COMMUNITIES	**CT1**	**Intermediates between C1a and T3a:**
	CT1a	**Myrtle and hard water fern:** myrtle with sassafras and leatherwood over hard water fern and manfern
	CT1b	**Myrtle with clear understoreys:** myrtle with sassafras and leatherwood over clear understoreys
	CT1c	**Myrtle and sassafras with open understoreys:** myrtle and sassafras and sometimes celery top pine over open understoreys or sporadic native laurel and/or sometimes native plum
	CT2	**Intermediates between C1a and T1a:**
	CT2a	**Myrtle and sassafras with horizontal:** myrtle and sassafras over horizontal with mother shield fern
	CT3	**Celery top pine and myrtle with clear understoreys:** celery top pine and myrtle over clear understoreys

WHERE TO SEE RAINFOREST

Note (1) "Nearest town" = population over 1000; (2) FC = Forestry Commission; (3) DLPW = Department of Lands, Parks and Wildlife

Locality/feature	Nearest town	Managing authority, enquiries	Remarks
NORTH-WEST			
Balfour Track Forest Reserve	Smithton	FC **Enquiries** District Forester, Smithton	Tall callidendrous and thamnic rainforest; walking track; access Blackwater Road
Celery top pine nature trail	Smithton	FC **Enquiries** District Forester, Smithton	Short walking track through rainforest with celery top pine and dense horizontal; access Tayatea Road
Hellyer Gorge State Reserve	Somerset	DLPW **Enquiries** DLPW Ranger, Rocky Cape	Callidendrous and thamnic rainforest; walking track; access Murchison Highway
Julius River Forest Reserve	Smithton	FC **Enquiries** District Forester, Smithton	Callidendrous and thamnic rainforest; walking track; access Sumac Road
Waldheim (Cradle Valley)	Ulverstone	DLPW **Enquiries** DLPW Ranger, Cradle Mountain	Thamnic rainforest with King Billy pine; some deciduous beech; walking tracks; access Cradle Mountain Road
Dismal Swamp	Smithton	FC/DLPW **Enquiries** District Forester, Smithton	Viewing point over Dismal Swamp; nature trail through blackwood swamp forest; access Bass Highway
NORTH			
Meander Forest Reserve	Deloraine	FC **Enquiries** District Forester, Deloraine	Callidendrous and thamnic rainforest with King Billy pine; walking tracks; access Meander Falls Road
Liffey Forest Reserve, Liffey Falls State Reserve	Deloraine	FC/DLPW **Enquiries** District Forester, Deloraine	Callidendrous rainforest; walking track; access Lake Highway
Pine Lake	Deloraine	DLPW **Enquiries** Crown Land Warden, Liawenee	Open montane rainforest with pencil pines; access Lake Highway
Quamby Forest Reserve	Deloraine	FC **Enquiries** District Forester, Deloraine	Callidendrous and thamnic rainforest; access Lake Highway
NORTH-EAST			
Mount Victoria Forest Reserve	Scottsdale	FC **Enquiries** District Forester, Scottsdale	Walking track through high altitude callidendrous rainforest; access Mount Albert Road

Weldborough Pass	——St Helens	DLPW **Enquiries** Crown Land Warden, St Helens	Callidendrous rainforest; access Tasman Highway

EAST

Meetus Falls Forest Reserve	Swansea	FC **Enquiries** District Forester, Triabunna	Relic patch of callidendrous sassafras-musk rainforest; access M Road via Lake Leake Highway

SOUTH

Hastings Cave State Reserve	Dover	DLPW **Enquiries** DLPW Ranger, Hastings Cave	Patches of thamnic and implicate rainforest amidst mixed forest; walking tracks; access Hastings Cave Road
Mount Field National Park	Maydena	DLPW **Enquiries** DLPW Ranger, Mount Field	Small patches of callidendrous, thamnic, implicate and open montane rainforest. Access Lake Dobson Road
Mount Mangana	South Bruny Island	FC **Enquiries** District Forester, Geeveston	Relic pockets of closed rainforest (callidendrous and thamnic); walking track; access Coolangatta Road
Scotts Peak Road	Maydena	FC/DLPW **Enquiries** DLPW Ranger, Mount Field; Norfolk District Forester, Hobart	Thamnic, callidendrous and implicate patches found near road from Frodshams Pass to Serpentinite Creek; nature trail
Tahune Forest Reserve	Geeveston	FC **Enquiries** District Forester, Geeveston	Riverine rainforest with Huon pine; walking tracks; access Arve Road

WEST

Bradshaws Road	Queenstown	Hydro-Electric Commission	Pockets of thamnic and implicate rainforest, including King Billy pine and deciduous beech
Gordon River State Reserve	Strahan	DLPW **Enquiries** DLPW Ranger, Strahan	Huon pine; gallery rainforest; access via boat from Strahan
Lyell Highway near Victoria Pass	Queenstown	DLPW **Enquiries** DLPW Ranger, Queenstown	Extensive thamnic, callidendrous and implicate rainforest found near highway between Victoria Pass and King William Saddle
Pieman Road	Tullah	DLPW	Extensive thamnic and callidendrous rainforest patches from Huskisson River to Stanley River
Pieman River State Reserve	Savage River	DLPW **Enquiries** DLPW Hobart	Riverine rainforest with Huon pine; walking trail; access Waratah Rd
Murchison Hwy	Rosebery	DLPW	Extensive areas of callidendrous and thamnic rainforest between Luina and Waratah